Free to Live

A Testament to a Great Adventure

by Joseph F. Girzone

Compiled by
Dorothy K. Ederer, O.P. and **Gary Riggi**

Acknowledgements

The unique cover is a photo from Dan Friedt,
a dear Canadian Friend.

There is no word to express my gratitude to Kelly Sandula-Gruner
for the exquisite job she continues to do on the cover.

Madeline Carino added her special touch again
by contributing the graphic design in the book.

Words can't express my gratitude to Chris Tremblay for helping
me with format and layout and his exquisite expertise in
proofreading this manuscript.

Foreword

This book is about
Fr. Joseph F. Girzone's life as a priest.

I hope you enjoy his wit,
his adventures
and his dedication to
Jesus!

Dorothy K. Ederer O.P.

Table of Contents

Chapter One

It may come as a surprise to people who know me, that I never wanted to be a pastor. I was content just doing my work in parishes, and accepting any assignment given to me by the pastor. It would seem to most people that being a pastor would be the fulfillment of a dream as a priest. It was not so with me. I dreaded becoming a pastor. A pastor represents the bishop and representing the bishop meant not putting the bishop in a compromising position in matters of church law, and protecting the bishop when difficult issues arose. I knew I would have no problem being loyal to the bishop and that I would always defend him in difficult situations, but when it came to being a shepherd to the people, I had grave concerns. I am not a holy man, I have struggled all my life trying to be a good priest, and it was most difficult. But, when it came to being a shepherd to the people, I was always uncompromising. To be a shepherd, which is what the word 'pastor' means, was the same as being modeled after the Good Shepherd. Since my years as a Carmelite friar, I had pondered how Jesus, the Good Shepherd, would treat people. I poured over the gospels day after day, trying to place Jesus in difficult situations in people's lives today. I always took seriously the Canon Law of the Church, and I knew I would have a very difficult time as a pastor when there would be situations in the lives of parishioners that would conflict with church law. What would

Jesus do, follow the law or show compassion for people struggling under very painful circumstances? I never wanted to be in that kind of a predicament, where I would feel compelled to make a decision that would be in opposition to Canon Law, which the bishop is expected to enforce, or in opposition to what I knew Jesus would do. For that reason, the thought of being a pastor was horrendous, because I knew that eventually I would end up in deep conflict with church officials, the one thing I dreaded.

So, when I received a phone call from the diocesan personnel director, telling me the bishop would like me to be pastor and asked me to consider it, I was very honest. I told him I was happy where I was. At the time, I was an assistant at St. Joseph's in Scotia, New York. It was a big parish, with a parish school, though most of the children attended public school. One of my responsibilities was to find volunteer teachers to teach religion to the almost 2000 children attending the public schools. Besides working in the parish, I had other responsibilities in the larger community which took much of my time.

The parish was a fun place and the people were most friendly. They were always open to new things. One lent I thought it would be nice to have a cross placed outside the church for Good Friday. I asked a contractor, Jerry Riggi, whose family were dear friends, if he would make one for us. He and his brother Gene had worked in their father's construction company since they were kids, and they could do anything. Jerry put together a life-size cross and brought it over to the rectory one day. "Okay, now what do we do with it?" He asked, then continued, "I'd like to crucify *you* on it to make it real for all you put me through." I laughed, because I knew I was always asking him to do things for me. I gave him three huge nails used to pin down railroad tracks, and asked if he would put them in place on the cross. Then, I asked if he would dig a hole off to the side in front of the entrance to the church, and hook up a flood light about five feet in front of the hole, all of which he did. The cross we kept in the back of the vestibule until Good Friday night. During the service Friday night, I had the maintenance man put the cross in place and turn the flood light on the cross, and drape a twenty foot piece of white plastic runner left over from a wedding, over the cross beam and hanging down on both sides of the central beam. Since there was a slight breeze at night, the runner swished in the wind, creating an eerie sound like the scene was alive. When the people came out of church into the darkness outside they were struck with this sight. It seemed so real, it gave many of them goose bumps.

Other good things happened in the parish. Another family, the Gatta family, were dear friends, one of the Gattas was married to my dentist, and the two families, the Gattas and the Coppolas comprised a good number of the parishioners. On Halloween, we dressed up in outlandish costumes and "terrorized" the neighborhood. One year we thought of making a coffin and floating it down the Mohawk River, then call the sheriff, Barney Waldron, who was a friend, and tell him there was a coffin floating down the

Mohawk. We finally decided against it, since Barney, who could also be a joker, might put us all in jail, just as a prank to get even.

So, when I was asked to consider being pastor, the thought of being transferred was not appealing at all. And it was a time when many things were changing in the church. The Second Vatican Council had tried to loosen up the tight hold the clergy had over the people, and even the tight hold the bishops had over priests, making church life much more relaxed than it had been in centuries. Parish life was starting to be fun. Even the priests were made to feel much freer and were no longer told they were going to be reassigned, but were asked and allowed to discuss a possible new assignment. We were no longer ordered to take an assignment, but were asked to consider the request.

Now that I had received this phone call from the bishop's office, I considered very thoroughly the prospect of being pastor, and as much as I would have liked to oblige, I felt it would not be a happy situation either for me or for the diocese. I was very honest, and told him I appreciated the offer but felt I could not accept. At that point, the truth about a gentler authority bared itself. It was no longer a matter for my consideration. The tone of the conversation changed, and I was told that if I did not cooperate, I would be sent out to the far end of the diocese in the spring. I then realized that the new policy was just talk, and that the bishop was probably having a hard time getting a priest to accept the assignment for some reason, and that I did not have a choice. I was mistaken in thinking things were changing. I was not nice at that point. I said, "Don't ever dare threaten me again, and tell the bishop the same thing. I had been a monk, and we did as we were told. I never had a problem with that, but don't make me think I have a choice, then threaten me if I don't go along. That's an insult. Tell the bishop that if he wants me to do something, all he has to do is tell me, and I will do it. But don't ever play this game with me again." The appointment was as pastor of Our Lady of Mount Carmel parish in Amsterdam, New York, and I was told when I was expected to be there.

I did have one other serious consideration. Although I had been an assistant to the pastor at Saint Joseph's for almost four years, I had other assignments outside the parish. One was with the Human Rights Commission, which appointment I reluctantly accepted only after the director, Dr. David Ben-Daniel, a nuclear physicist, approached the bishop and requested that he use his 'influence' to get me to accept the appointment. I had always felt the Commission was too liberal and not practical in the way they attempted to resolve critical public issues. Ben-Daniel knew I worked well in complex community situations. The bishop told me to accept the appointment as member of the Human Rights Commission.

Hardly a week after my appointment to the Commission there was a riot in the local jail, and I was told by the County Manager that it was my responsibility to negotiate with the inmates and settle the matter. The situation in the jail was worse than I thought. A very liberal priest had been encouraging the inmates to protest that their rights were being violated by the jail administration. They had been preparing their protest for quite a while. For weeks, they had been sneaking small boxes of raisins as well as packages of sugar out of the dining room to make wine in a pail they kept hidden in one of the empty cells. The day of the riot, they had been drinking, and subsequently rioted and took over the jail. I knew nothing about jails and what goes on inside those places. I soon got a crash course. When I went to the jail, I found that the sheriff and the deputies had all fled and called the police. The inmates had taken over the facility and the officials were concerned about the female prisoners. When I entered the office, the District Attorney and an Episcopal priest were talking to the inmates and the three inmates were becoming more and more agitated. After two hours, they were unable to make any headway. I told the District Attorney that the County Manager had sent me over and that it was my responsibility to handle the problem. He and the priest gladly left, and I sat down and tried to reason with the three spokesmen for the inmates.

The first question they asked me was, "Aren't you afraid to be in here alone with us?" I said no, because I was the only hope they had of getting the problems resolved, and they could either be reasonable and trust me, or we would get nowhere, and the alternatives could be a nightmare. At that point, two policemen came in with guns drawn, and the inmates got upset all over again.

"You see, Father, why we can't get anywhere; these guys and their guns." I asked the police to leave which they reluctantly did, as they were concerned about my safety. I assured them that I would be all right.

After a rather lengthy discussion and promising that I personally would begin a thorough investigation of the jail conditions, the inmates' negotiating team agreed to have all the inmates return to their cells and get ready for supper which I promised I would arrange with the sheriff. So, I went up into the cell block with the three men while they talked the rest of the inmates to return to their cells. I again assured them all that I would begin an investigation immediately.

The ensuing investigation took three difficult months, with the sheriff's deputies supporting the inmates and giving me the most damaging information about conditions, and though the final report was an indictment of the county's irresponsibility for the deplorable conditions, the county board of representatives, after assigning a committee of lawyers to investigate my report, agreed that the Commission's findings, though extremely embarrassing, were accurate and that the recommendations should be implemented as soon as possible. Since that time there is now a new jail over three times the size of the original one. What gave credibility to our investigation was our little committee which consisted of only three people, Ken Buhrmaster, the founder and chairman of a chain of Scotia National Banks in our area, and a man with a sterling reputation. The other member of the committee was a former inmate, Gordon Collier, who had the trust of the inmates, and was a great help in interpreting information we collected from the jail staff and the inmates. I felt that combination was all I needed for credibility with both sides of the issue in the community.

Work with the Commission did not end there. Shortly after the riot in the jail, serious disturbances in the Schenectady public school system shook the community. A white high school student came to school one morning with an ax hidden inside his overcoat. At the same time the front porch of a black member of the Commission was dynamited. The president of the school board, Richard Della Ratta, felt that the Commission was the only government agency competent enough, and with enough respect and creditability in the community to handle the situation objectively and conduct the investigation in a fair and impartial manner. That investigation and findings took well over six very difficult and stressful months. When the hearings were over, we were left with hundreds of pages of testimony and documents. Writing the report from this massive amount of material took many hours late into many nights, when I stayed up till two and three o'clock in the morning trying to put the report together in a way that made sense, and would be acceptable to the community. Finally, after certain changes were made to obtain the final approval of the whole Commission, the document was presented to the President of the School Board and to the press. The press was most helpful in that the local paper serialized the full report over a thirty-day period, which gave the whole community the chance to ponder over many irresponsible community attitudes on both sides of the racial issues which were the root causes of the continuing sporadic racial crises in the community. No community group escaped censure for their share in the dangerously explosive tensions which could easily have ended in loss of life, which, thank God, did not happen. One important effect of the report was its wide repercussions, which brought about a dramatic change in the discipline system throughout the New York State public schools.

During this time, the stress had taken its effect on me, and I felt I needed to get away from everything. All this work plus the difficulties in the parish at that time were taking their toll. The diocese had been offering sabbaticals to priests at the time, so they could spend six months in Rome or other important international centers for retreats and continuing studies in theology. I felt it was something I desperately needed at the time, so I sent in my application. A few days later I received the diocese' response, "We would like to offer this to you, but it is for priests who are in important positions where they can influence large numbers of people." If those were not the exact words, they are close. When I showed the pastor, who was a canon lawyer in the diocese, he just laughed quietly as if he did not expect anything different from the diocese. So, to avoid getting depressed, I threw myself even more strenuously into my work.

One issue that surfaced during the school investigation was low income housing. Rapidly deteriorating conditions of old homes in the area where most of the poor were living was a contributing cause of the unrest. The conservative politicians in Schenectady who were in power, were opposed to low income housing. Unfortunately, vast millions of dollars, tied to acceptance of low income housing, were lost to the community because of an ineffective City Council, and a downright ignorant Mayor's refusal to provide the housing. By that time, I was the Chairman of the Human Rights Commission, and I invited the mayor and city council members to a Commission hearing. By the end of the discussion, we asked if the Mayor and City Council could pick their own sites for low income housing, would they be willing to accept low income housing, which was badly needed, and which would open the floodgates for massive influx of funds to renovate the city. They said they would.

With that agreement, I went to Washington, D.C. to talk to the director of HUD, and after talking to him for almost an hour, he agreed to make an exception, the only one ever granted, to allow the Mayor and City Council to pick their own sites for the low-income housing. Delighted at the success of the trip, I came back and reported the good news to the Commission and to the Mayor. The Mayor then chose the sites, and the sites were approved by the City Council. That took place on a Friday afternoon.

14

The Saturday morning paper's headline read, "GE Protests use of Sites for Low Income Housing." Since Dr. Ben-Daniel worked for GE, I phoned him immediately and asked what it was all about. He said he had already considered it, and found out that the Mayor had called GE the previous afternoon and asked if GE could use those sites for a parking lot. When the GE official said, "Yes," the Mayor then told the GE official to call the newspaper and protest the city's choice of those sites for housing, which he promptly did. So, the Mayor scuttled the whole project and in his great 'wisdom,' forfeited hundreds of millions of federal funds which the city could have used, especially since GE moved out shortly afterwards and left the area not only with a loss of thousands of jobs, but with a loss of hundreds of millions of dollars in tax revenue from GE, which forced a massive increase in property taxes.

This happened at the same time as the bishop wanted me to be a pastor, which I felt was irresponsible on his part. It was a difficult time for me as I felt the bishop had made a commitment to the County when he told me to take the position on the Commission, a commitment which I still felt obligated to fulfill as best as I could, even with my new responsibilities as pastor.

It was only a few days later that I took up my assignment as pastor of Our Lady of Mount Carmel in Amsterdam, New York, twelve miles away. The rectory was a beautiful home that had belonged to a well-to-do businessman. It had been moved to the present site on the church property, and was a very comfortable residence. The

15

former pastor, who could be very crude in the way he treated people, was now a canon lawyer attached to the chancery, but there was a priest in residence whose assignment was as a teacher at the local Catholic High School. I had known Father Randall Patterson for years as his family lived in a parish where I had been stationed at one time. He was a big help to me when needed for Mass on Sunday, though he was not assigned to other parish duties. He enjoyed doing his friends' weddings which relieved me of some of those responsibilities.

I spent my first week at the parish trying to comprehend what was involved. Besides the church and the school which had just been closed, there was the rectory and the convent, which was vacant and still had a mortgage. There was also a parish cemetery located nine miles from the parish. The maintenance man, Tony Simiele, who had emigrated from Italy, was a skilled mechanic and most helpful and supportive of all that I had to do in the parish. Besides taking care of the parish buildings, he also was the caretaker of the cemetery. There was also a remarkable lady who did the cooking and kept the rectory immaculate. Her name was Lena Brignole. She and the maintenance man, Tony Simiele, were the only parish employees at the time.

What shocked me the first week I was there was that there was no parish secretary. This I found hard to believe, as there was no one who could explain to me the financial condition of the parish. The only financial records were two saving account books with deposit and withdrawal entries, but with no notes on parish expenses. There was a check book with few entries. There was also a special savings account for the cemetery which amounted to, if I am not mistaken, approximately $30,000 which was legally committed to the perpetual care of the cemetery grounds. At the time the total amount of money available in the parish account for parish expenses was about $6,000. It was my first big letdown. There was also money from bingo, which could vary from week to week. Gambling was not something I approved of as a way of financing a Christian community, although without it the parish would have had to close long before I arrived there.

I had no idea what kind of financial reports the previous pastor sent to the chancery, since there were no parish records. Whatever reports were sent had to have been favorable, as the diocese thought the parish had considerably more money than it did.

There was a small organ in the loft of the church but it was not very dependable. I found that out at the first Saturday evening Mass. That Mass was my introduction to the parish and to the handful of parishioners who attended that Mass. When I went out into the sanctuary to begin Mass, my heart sank. There were fewer than a hundred, mostly saintly older Italian women, and a handful of older Italian men. They soon became very dear friends, and I enjoyed their quaint Italian-accented English, and they smiled when I tried to talk to them in Italian. Those people remained dear friends up to this day, at least those who have survived.

The next day, Sunday, there were three Masses scheduled, 7:30, 9:00 and 11:00. I took the first and the last Mass, and Father Patterson offered the 9:00 o'clock Mass. After the 7:30 Mass, there were two parish societies, the St. Anthony Society and the Mount Carmel Men's Society, who had their meetings at that time, but each on alternating Sundays. Those meetings I always tried to attend. I enjoyed those down-to-earth happy gentlemen. It was only after attending several of their meetings that I began to realize that, even though on the surface they seemed to take the meetings seriously, they conducted discussions in the most solemn manner, but, always with tongue in cheek, which they all knew, but which totally eluded me for almost three years. They all knew it. I was the only one who took them seriously. I am sure they had their amusing tales that circulated around the parish about their keeping me in the dark as to what was going on. I must admit, I was completely taken in, but it was all in good fun, and I loved those guys. They were the heart of the parish, as least as far as the men were concerned. Though they were mostly in their sixties and seventies, they did the cooking for most of the parish affairs, and made the parish an exciting and fun place to experience.

Chapter Two

My top priority was to learn about the parishioners, their names, their background, where they worked, who was related to whom, their attitudes towards the parish. It did not take long to realize there were two groups of Italians in the city, and two Italian parishes. The other parish was Saint Michael's, a wealthy parish attended by mostly professional families and well-to-do business people. Our parish consisted mostly of former rug factory workers, who had lost their jobs when Mohawk Carpets and other rug companies moved to the southern states. The parishioners lived for the most part on Social Security checks, which were meager since they were based on previously low salaries. Almost ninety percent of the parish lived on Social Security, which explained why the Sunday donations were minimal, though, like the widow's mite in the gospel, were an expression of considerable sacrifice on the part of these good people. The total Sunday collections were a little over five hundred dollars, which amounted to roughly $25,000 a year. I began to understand that the parishioners probably needed help more from the parish than the parish needed from them, but they were a proud and dignified people and lived comfortably with their frugal life style.

At the time, I was still carrying responsibilities to the Human Rights Commission in Schenectady, trying to resolve the low-income housing issue. Another responsibility, which sprung from my commission work, was my membership on the Advisory Board for the State Office on Aging, resulting from my investigation of an elderly married couple who froze to death after their electricity had been shut off by the power company because they forgot to pay their bill. As an offshoot of that, the county established an Office on Aging. At the most recent State meeting I learned that Montgomery County, the county where our parish was located, had the highest percentage of senior citizens in all of New York State, and there was no Office on Aging in the county. That was beyond my belief.

What amazed me about the parishioners was how they were able to survive on so little income, and how they ever managed to own their own homes, which were modest but well-constructed and very well kept. Most of the people were involved in construction of some kind or other, even if they were experienced amateurs. Many of the families were from the same towns in Italy and were close friends, even if not closely related. They helped each other and managed to survive even in most difficult times.

That they remained loyal to the Church impressed me as they were never treated well by the bishops, and by several of their pastors, who were not Italian, and who often socialized with people in other parts of the city. For years, they had no church of their own where they could worship. The bishop at the time told them to worship at Saint Michael's. But, that was across the river and up on a hill. They would have to walk the distance of perhaps three miles, and then back home, and in the hot summers and brutal winters that was extremely difficult. Also, the upper-class Italians did not want to be associated with these people, whom they referred to as 'animals without tails', which my new parishioners enjoyed telling me with no trace of animosity. Feeling not just unwelcome but, unwanted, they eventually stopped going to that church, but remained loyal to their Catholic faith.

One of the families in the parish had a relative in Italy who was a priest. When he came over to the States for a visit, he was asked to stay and be their priest since they had none. The people promised to take care of him. He consented, and they now had a priest, but not in good standing because the whole procedure was done without the bishop's approval. Eventually the parishioners built their own church and the priest lived in the bell tower, from what I was told, though that is hard to believe, as the priest's relatives in the parish were respectable people. He did have a difficult life, however, and died at a relatively young age.

Finally, the bishop established a parish on the South Side, which was what the neighborhood was called, referring to the time when it was the old city dump. Eventually a new church had to be constructed, as the old church was totally inadequate. One of the men's groups in the neighborhood owned a large tract of land up on a higher elevation from where most of the people lived. The society donated the land to the parish for the construction of the church. To encourage generous donations for the construction the pastor and diocesan officials had an architect draw up plans with an artist's rendering of a quaint European Italian style church to remind them of their childhood memories in their home towns in Italy.

As the building was being constructed, the men went up to the site each day to watch the progress. Italian men are by nature either amateur architects or theoretical contractors. Soon they would have their new church just like they remembered back home in Italy. The further along the construction went, the less the building looked like the artist's rendering, and besides that, there was a long extended structure going off the back of the church. When they asked the pastor what that thing was, he told them that that was the school. Not only did the church have not the slightest resemblance to what they had been told, but they felt a school had been foisted on them by the diocese in an underhanded manner. They felt the bishop had deceived them and they felt insulted. From that point on they could never trust bishops.

Furious, the men told the whole rest of the parish that the bishop had pulled another fast one on them. Deeply hurt by what they felt was a betrayal and an insult to their good will, the vast majority of the parishioners vowed never to support the school. The pastor at the time was a very saintly man, and the people loved him dearly, and never cast any blame on him for what had happened. However, they never supported the school. Years later, they still had blessed memories of that priest, though they never again trusted a bishop or chancery officials. To them they were either crooks or incompetent. From then on their pastors had to walk a tight rope in their relationship between the parishioners and the bishop's office.

As soon as the construction was finished, the church was blessed and opened for services. So was the school. A small number of younger parishioners with families wanted to send their children to a Catholic school, so they assumed the whole financial burden for the school, and its expenses, and for the convent where the nuns were to live. The school thrived for a number of years, at the cost of great sacrifice to the handful of dedicated young families, though as time went on it became most difficult to maintain. The number of students was hardly over a hundred and though the supporters were willing to keep working hard, the diocese felt it was more prudent to close it. The parishioners requested the diocese to help them financially to keep the facility open, but were told they were not in the business of financing schools. The school was finally closed just before I was assigned there as pastor.

My first crisis occurred only a few weeks after my assignment. The parishioners who were loyal to the school were very upset with the diocese. They told me in no uncertain terms that that was the end of their fundraising activities. Though their children were now transferred to the Irish parish school as they called Saint Mary's, they were not at all happy with the autocratic way it was done. They were all kind to me and understood there was nothing I could do, but I still felt the resentment that remained for the whole time of my assignment to the parish.

It was not long before I received a call from the diocese that the bishop and his whole chancery staff, plus the administrators from the diocesan school office would be holding a meeting with the seven pastors of Amsterdam. The meeting was held in our closed school. The bishop was there with all the top officials from the chancery and the diocesan school office.

The upshot of the meeting was that each parish was to support Saint Mary's school where all the children were now attending. The amount each parish would pay would be pro-rated on the number of students attending Saint Mary's from each parish. Since Mount Carmel had the most, with a hundred students. We were assessed $25,000. The assessment of the other parishes was at most $2500, and they were much better off financially. When I tried to explain that $25,000 was the total annual income from Sunday collections, the bishop commented that since there were no longer any school expenses I should use the money we saved by not having a school. I explained that we still had the school building and the convent mortgage, and the heat bills and maintenance expenses for those buildings, and that the loyal school committee refused to work on any fundraising programs since the school was closed. And we still had to pay the salaries of the maintenance man and the parish cook and housekeeper. I said as nicely as I could that I could not in conscience come up with that kind of money. Besides our parishioners were elderly and poor, and the parish had to help them in whatever little ways we could. One school official scoffed at my saying that I was concerned about the old folks, which showed his ignorance. There was no way I could agree with what the bishop demanded, and said that what he was asking would destroy the parish. The only pastor who supported me was an old German pastor, Father Beck, who, strangely, retired a few weeks later. The bishop was so upset with my refusal to go along, he ended the meeting and told the pastors to figure out some solution on their own, and get back to him.

The other pastors had a meeting without me and called me afterwards, saying that they could not afford the assessment, and asked if they could count on me to support a firm stand at the meeting with the chancellor. I promised I would. When that meeting took place, they all caved in when they were asked individually; even the dean who had called me. However, I kept my word, and stood firm. That hurt, but it taught me a lesson, that I should never trust people, even fellow priests, to stand by you in difficult situations. My fears of being a pastor were now a bitter reality, as I was already obnoxious to the bishop and the chancery office, and as one official told me later, the frequent butt of table talk at the chancery lunch.

But, at the parish, I could not afford to let myself become obsessed with what the bishop and the chancery officials thought of me. I kept myself focused on building up the parish. I could not help falling in love with the gentle, good, fun-loving people in this parish. They later were to become the characters in my original "Joshua," and were just like I described them in the book. I was beginning to learn something that I never paid much attention to before, and that was that church officials seemed to have no idea of people as Jesus' hurting, troubled, and damaged sheep. This was becoming more and more clear. My people had been hurt so much by insensitive priests, and bishops. One incident in particular the people told me about really upset me. The former pastor was offering the funeral Mass for an elderly lady. At the offertory time, the altar boy forgot to take the stoppers out of the glass cruets containing the water and wine. The pastor impatiently kicked the altar boy in the shin to the shock of the congregation who were the family of the altar boy, whose grandmother was being buried. The people never forgot the incident, and it bothered them deeply especially when they found out that right after the incident, the bishop appointed that priest to the diocesan tribunal as one of the diocesan officials because he had a doctorate in Canon Law.

Seeing what kind and generous people the parishioners were, and so painfully aware of all they had suffered for their faith over the years, I was determined to put my whole heart and soul into bringing these people to a level where they could feel proud of themselves, and have a good feeling about the Church again. They were not always easy to deal with because they had been hurt so often. And in the beginning, I had to prove myself, and show them that I cared for them. They told me that other pastors used to befriend people of other local parishes, but never got close to their own parishioners.

The first funeral was an eye opener. The man who drove me to the cemetery said hardly any other pastor survived more than a couple of years, and that after sizing me up, said that he would give me six months. I laughed. "Six months! Hell, you people are a pushover; I'll just be starting then." We eventually became good friends. In fact, at his mother's funeral, a short time later, which was huge, people came from all over. He felt bad we could not have nice music at his mother's funeral, so on his own he announced in the local newspaper that the family requested donations be made to a pipe organ fund in lieu of flowers or Mass cards, so the parish could have a least an organ that reminded the parishioners of the old country. I could not believe he could do such a thing without letting me know beforehand, as there was no way we could ever afford a pipe organ. I also knew that the chancery office would be even more upset at such a venture, especially since I had told them that the parish was poor.

In the end I was shocked to find out that people who would donate five or ten dollars for a Mass, or a bit more for flowers, would donate forty, fifty dollars towards the pipe organ fund. In less than a year, to my surprise, the fund had close to $48,000. Andy Gigliotti, a funeral director in Albany, and a dear friend, arranged with a good friend of his, Leonard Carlson, who built pipe organs, to use a sixteen-rank organ discarded from another parish, and with approval from the vice-chancellor of the diocese who was encouraging parishes to have pipe organs, install it in Mount Carmel. It turned out to be a gorgeous piece of workmanship, complete with a rank of trumpets protruding from the front. The whole organ was installed against the wall behind the altar, so when people came into the church they were struck with this beautiful work of art facing them. After it was installed the parishioners were so proud and thrilled. There was nothing like it in the whole city.

The problem now was we had no organist who could play it. And the parish had no money to pay for an organist. By this time, I had been struggling to put the parish financial situation on a business-like basis. I just could not work with two savings account books. Not long after my being in the parish, I asked a wonderful lady, named Gilda Libertucci, if she would be my secretary and take care of the finances. Her husband, John Libertucci, worked for one of the major computer corporations. We had become dear friends. They had three beautiful children. Once Gilda started to work, I told her that it was essential that every one of the diocesan financial regulations be scrupulously observed. I could tell she was just what the parish needed, and in no time at all, had all the parish finances in perfect order. Within six months, she had already established a remarkable bookkeeping system, and with her passion for accuracy, accounted for every penny that came in and went out of the parish. On a couple of occasions, she could not account for something like fifteen or eighteen cents. I took that amount out of my pocket and gave it to her. She looked at me shocked. "I can't do that. Don't worry, Father, I will take the books home and go over everything again until I find my mistake." Next morning, she came in with a big smile. I knew what it meant. "I told you I'd find it," was all she said. We probably had under her efficient care, the most accurate and honest financial records in the whole diocese. I had insisted that every penny be accounted for, and everything would be completely, as they say today, transparent.

Angelo, the fellow who started the pipe organ fund, never realized the problem he raised for me. I had been trying to convince the chancery office that the parish was poor. And it was. Most of the donations for the pipe organ came from people out of town and other parts of Amsterdam, many of them Protestant and Jewish friends. However, as I found later, even though our financial records were so honest, the diocese did not believe that our parish was poor. They also most likely had inaccurate financial reports from prior to my assignment to the parish.

The pipe organ fund was so successful, the parishioners, as well as I, immediately realized that that was the way to strengthen the financial situation in the parish, and a very creative way to keep the parish financially viable. It also made it possible for the parish to entertain ways of helping people in need.

But, this fund and other funds that followed were in a special legal category. I had not realized it at the time we set them up, but they had to be legally separate from all other parish income. People made those donations for a very special reason which was legally binding on the parish, and that money had to be used for the specific purpose for which the people donated that money. So, as soon as money started coming in, Gilda set up separate accounts to keep those moneys separate from ordinary parish income, which alone could be used to cover parish expenses.

Through the eyes of the diocesan accountants, however, they saw things differently. Diocesan assessments on parish income could not legally include money in the various funds, so to their way of thinking, I was dishonestly depriving the diocese of money that could be theirs. But, that was not my intention. Since I could not expect much money from our elderly parishioners, it was just our way of tapping sources from outside the parish to help the parish grow. At the beginning, I never considered any of these other issues involved, as this was all so new to me. But, later, when I found out the legal ramifications of the various funds, I could understand why the diocese was suspicious. At the same time, I was delighted, and so were the people, when they realized that that money had to stay in the parish and had be used only for what the donors intended. This gave the people a tremendous satisfaction. However, the whole issue was soon to come to a head.

Chapter Three

Though I was now firmly entrenched in my parish, I still had unfinished business with the Human Rights Commission. One of the most stressful unresolved issues was the restless conditions in the state prisons. I had no direct involvement or legal competence to handle these situations, but some of the former inmates in the Schenectady County jail were eventually given long sentences to the state prison system, particularly, Dannamora, way up in Clinton County near the Canadian border. These fellows had appreciated the thoroughness of our investigation of the jail situation, so they passed my name around to the inmates at Dannamora. Whenever there was a disturbance or talk of a riot, rather than go through the hell of a riot in the big prisons which could be costly, even of human life, they would contact their lawyers and ask them to request that I go up to intervene and try to work out a resolution to situations before they turned into a full-blown confrontations or violent riots.

This was very stressful work, as I felt inadequate and always went to the place with fear and trepidation. I had gone on several trips while I was in my previous parish assignment, and I knew the pastor did not particularly appreciate it, but how could I refuse when there was so much at stake. But, now that I was a pastor and had responsibilities in my parish, I had to be more creative in resolving prison tensions in a way that could be more permanent. The last time I was called, I contacted the State Commissioner of

Correction and told him that the inmates' lawyers had contacted me, telling me that there was a tense situation at breakfast that morning. The Commissioner said that he had been talking to the warden earlier in the day, and was told that everything was quiet and that nothing unusual was happening. But, the Commissioner said he would call there again and get back to me, which he did. "You were right, Father, there was an incident this morning but they did not tell me about it earlier. I think it would be a good idea if you do go up. I'm beginning to realize they are not upfront with me, and I am having a hard time finding out what's really going on in these places. Call me as soon as you get back. I'd appreciate it."

With the Commissioner's support, I drove the hundred and some miles up through the Adirondack Mountains, to the prison, and was made to wait in the warden's outer office for well over an hour. But, I refused to be put off. I told the warden I would wait as long as I had to, since the Commissioner was most interested in what I had to report. With that he allowed me to enter the cell blocks and the solitary confinement area where the hardcore prisoners were kept, men who had been transferred from Attica after the infamous riot and massacre there when the National Guard was sent in to quell an uprising the previous year, at great loss of life. These dangerous prisoners were kept in solitary confinement, in a most depressing underground prison which reminded me of an ante-chamber to hell. There were no windows and the inmates were totally isolated. It could easily drive people to insanity.

When the other prisoners in the general population heard that I had gone down to the lower level, they asked me, "You're not going to try to move them up with us, are you, Father? They're animals. We're all scared of those guys. Don't let them be put in with the general population." After calming their fears, I went about talking to various inmates to try to get the information I needed.

After interviewing a number of them in an attempt to find out what had happened to provoke the tension at breakfast, I finally got the information I needed. One of the inmates who acted as a self-educated lawyer, did legal research for all the other inmates. He was respected and loved by all the inmates, because he was the only hope for many of them who were too poor to retain a lawyer. He had already helped many of them with their appeals. On the evening before, he had asked for permission to go to the library to do research. While conducting the inmate to the library, the officer did a strip search, intended to antagonize, and 'goosed' the fellow with his night stick. The inmate turned and slugged the officer which was just what the officer wanted, and which gave him the pretext he needed to put the fellow in solitary. Word of the incident spread through the whole prison overnight, and by morning the place was like an agitated beehive. They were not going to let this pass even if they had to have a major riot. These inmates' loyalty to one another, especially to one who stuck his own neck out for them, could be ferocious, as I found out before. There could be no stopping them once they made up their minds. They cared nothing about what would happen to themselves. They were men without hope or anything to live for. Dying for a friend was a mark of honor.

After I got my information, I started back to the warden's office. The captain on that shift was on his way out, and we walked together. I asked him some 'innocent' questions. The inmates had been complaining that letters to and from their lawyers are opened and read beforehand, and that they do not receive their newspapers. One of the questions I asked the captain was, "Why would the inmates complain about lawyers' letters being opened by the front office, and about not getting their newspapers? Is this something new? Are these just new complaints?" The captain was caught off guard. These were touchy issues for local prison officials, as they were part of the new reforms which were ordered implemented months before. Annoyed at my raising such a prickly issue, he lost his cool and his thoughtless response that followed was just what I needed, because it told me why there were so many problems at that facility. He blurted out, "Those 'assholes' in Albany aren't going to tell us how to run prisons? We'll run this place anyway we damn please."

I said nothing. By that time, we were at the warden's office and after thanking him for his courtesy and cooperation, I left and drove back through the mountains down to Amsterdam. After such a stressful experience, I had a difficult time keeping awake on the lonely country roads, but, thank God I made it home safely. One of the memories of that prison I will always treasure was viewing a huge painting in a large room reserved for paintings and articles made by the inmates, and which were for sale. This painting was at least nine feet high and six feet wide, of the crucifixion, done by an inmate. Christ was fastened to the cross, but the cross was not made of wood. It made of stone. The stone was broken and on close examination a viewer could see that the stone were tablets of the Ten Commandments. Jesus was crucified by our violation of God's laws. The painting was awesome, the features so beautiful and artistically perfect that thinking of it even years afterwards brings tears to my eyes. I wished at the time that I had money to buy it.

Another thing about Dannamora, was a story told by a priest who had been chaplain there. He said that there was an inmate who stayed by himself all the time. He attended Mass every Sunday, and whenever Mass was offered. As the priest got to know him from conversations he had with him, he soon realized that this fellow had a profound relationship with God. He expressed the most beautiful thoughts about God, and life, and his concern for his fellow inmates. As his understanding of the man deepened, he realized that the man had become over his many years there, a real saint, who, the priest was convinced, was having authentic mystical experiences of God's presence.

Once I got home, I didn't sleep well that night. Next morning, I called the Commissioner, and made my report, and included what I had been told by the captain of the guards. He replied without a moment's hesitation, "Father, I am grateful for what you have done. I wondered what was going on in these places. It is difficult to get a handle on situations as I have no way of telling if the wardens are being honest with me. But, after what you have said, I now know what must be done. I am sending not one inspector-general, but two inspectors-general, to go through that place with a fine-tooth comb. I intend to make that place the showcase for all the new reform regulations."

That was the last time that I had to do that kind of work, for which I was most grateful. There was more than enough work to be done in the parish, and much less stressful. Final closure to that experience occurred many years later, after I had retired. My brother Jim was in the hospital for a sextuple heart bypass. He called one day and told me there was a patient in the room with him who was dying and who knew me, and would appreciate a visit. He said he used to be the warden at Dannamora prison years ago. I went to the hospital that evening, visited my brother, and then went over to the warden's bed. I recognized him immediately but now he was only a shadow of the big man he used to be.

I asked him how he was coming along. "I'm in bad shape, Father. I appreciate your visit. I remember you. You are a good priest, Father."

"I try, John, but don't always succeed. Life is very complicated and in our work it is often difficult to know just what we should do. I know you can appreciate that."

"That is what I found in my job, too. It was always difficult, and we never knew what was right."

"I am sure you did your best," I said to him. "You had a difficult job in a most difficult place. Be at peace. That's all over and forgotten, even by God." After saying some prayers with him, I gave him my blessing, kissed him on the forehead and left. "Thanks, Father. Pray for me." "I will, John, and please pray for me, too."

I kissed my brother goodnight and left. It was a sad drive home, with my mind flooded with so many memories of so many horribly difficult times. I was beginning to realize that being a priest means carrying people's pain and burdens with you all your life.

Though the prison visits were over, there were still other issues from the past that played a part in my parish. While in Schenectady, two elderly people died after the power company had turned off their electricity a day or two before. They were both confined to wheel chairs, and died holding each other's hand. I had to investigate the situation and made my report. Then, as head of the Commission, I appointed a group to visit seniors in various parts of the county to see in what kind of conditions the elderly were living. When the staff came back and made their reports, we were all flabbergasted. Many of the elderly, even well-to-do elderly, some of whom were widows of GE executives, were living by themselves in mansions, with hardly any food in their houses. Some were forgetful, and in various stages of dementia. Many had no one to shop for them and had had few if any visitors for long periods of time. Many were malnourished and in frail condition. Our report was made to the County Board of Representatives. The chairman of the board was a decent person and asked what I would recommend. I told him that the best thing to do, as there were federal funds available for it, was to establish a county office on aging. To give him credit, and the board as well, they set up an office on aging within a matter of weeks, and had all the programs in place including the congregate meal sites for senior citizens so they could gather for lunch and companionship. These became very popular. A program to deliver hot lunch and a supper snack to the shut-ins was organized. Since then that office has saved the lives of thousands of elderly who ordinarily would have died of what the newspaper would have termed 'natural causes,' but, which was really starvation, and the effects of loneliness.

If ever an area needed an Office on Aging, it was where I was now, Montgomery County, including Amsterdam. I wrote a letter to the chairman of the Montgomery County Board of Representatives explaining my experiences in Schenectady. He was sympathetic, but was reluctant to use taxpayers' money for old people; their families can take care of them. This was something I was not going to take easily. If people in Schenectady had been living in life-threatening conditions, it was worse in Montgomery County, which was a sprawling rural county, with a much higher percentage of frail elderly, unable to shop and living alone in isolated places out on back roads through forests and desolate places.

God shows us at the most awesome times that he is a real partner when we are trying to do his work. It happened at about that time that the State had taken over the Orthodox Jewish Synagogue to build a highway, and did not reimburse the members with enough money to rebuild. Mount Carmel's parish council met one evening and the subject of the synagogue was brought up. "Father, you have been telling us that our work as Christians is not in the parish, but that we are the salt of the earth, and the yeast in the dough, and that we should do things to better the community at large."

"Which means what?" I asked. "What are you leading up to?"

"Well, if you really mean that, and also if you also meant it when you told us that you wanted us to make decisions, what about taking a vote to see how many would like to start a fundraising drive to help the Jews rebuild their synagogue?"

Totally caught off guard, I had to think for a minute, and then realized all I could say was, "Well, if that's what you decide, I will be proud of you." Now these were all tough guys, certainly not in the slightest bit liberal, but genuinely good people.

The vote was unanimous to go ahead and do it. They sent a letter to Rabbi Bloom telling him about the parish's decision. The following Sunday our whole parish was notified in the parish bulletin. The next day the headline in the Amsterdam "Recorder," read "Catholic Parish Starts Campaign to Rebuild Synagogue." The editor of the paper was Brad Broyles and I think he enjoyed the goings on at Mount Carmel. I think now most of my "Joshua" readers already know Brad, from talking to him when they call to speak to me at Joshua in Altamont, New York. We have been dear friends for the past 35 years. Brad became a Methodist minister.

The repercussions were immediate. I got two telephone calls from the Jewish community. The first one was from Rabbi Bloom, telling me how deeply touched his people were over the kindness of their friends at Mount Carmel. He also said that after his people were notified about our offer, fruit that had been hanging on the tree for years, finally started falling, so they probably will have enough pledges from their own people to build their synagogue. Then he asked if I would accept an invitation to give the dedication address when it was built. I told him I would be honored.

The next phone call was from Marc Breier, the chairman of the County Board of Representatives, who just happened to be the chairman of the finance committee for the synagogue. He told me I had put him in an embarrassing position, by offering to help build their synagogue when he had been so reluctant to help me when I asked him about an Office on Aging. I just laughed, and told him not to be embarrassed, but just to go along with me. He said, "I would like to offer you a deal. If your parish would be willing to run the County Office on Aging, and hire the director and the employees, I will have the county authorize the parish to be the official sponsor for the whole program. And we will help you."

"Marc, that's a deal."

We have been friends ever since. And after all the official papers were filled out and signed, Our Lady of Mount Carmel parish became the sponsor for the Office on Aging. One little mistake I made in filling out the papers. There was a question on the application requesting the name of the minority group in the demographics of the county. I thought it meant the nationality of the group with the smallest number of people in the community, so I put down, "Irish." Two days later I got a phone call from one of my Irish friends in the State Office on Aging, telling me that that Irish are not considered a minority group. "But, they are here in Amsterdam," I responded. "But, that is not what the document means." So, they changed it to Costa Ricans, after we both had a good laugh over my referring to the Irish as a minority group.

Once the approval came, we had to figure out where to get the local share of funding so we could qualify for the federal and state funding available. In this the state officials were a big help. As I had many friends there, from being on their advisory board, they made very practical suggestions which we very readily put into action. We had an excellent kitchen in the basement of the school building which was hardly ever used, except for occasional parish spaghetti suppers, and bingo on one night a week. We made that a congregate meal site for the seniors, and the rent we received from the State for that could be applied to the local share of funding required. We also started to use the school building for classes so we could earn more funds for our local share needed. I felt it was important for Americans to learn Russian and Chinese, so I tried to get teachers for those two languages, but was able to find only one to teach Russian. The College of Saint Rose in Albany rented a number of rooms for outreach classes which they wanted to conduct in the area. With the help of some talented ceramic teachers, we also set up a not-for-profit ceramic operation which was a great help in raising funds for our Office on Aging. Also, the parish council established a fund to help the elderly, which helped.

Next we needed people to run the Office on Aging. From experience, I felt I could trust a woman to be more concerned about all the minute details needed for the director's position. There was a lady in the parish who had a responsible position in an important local business. Her name was Carmela Simiele, the aunt of my maintenance man. From knowing her in the parish, and acquainted with her efficiency, I asked her if she would like the position as director. She was thrilled that I asked. A few weeks later, after resigning from her job, she was ready to start things moving. We also needed a few more workers, but we had to move slowly to make sure we had enough money to pay reasonable salaries. This was a critical issue for me, as I had had painful experiences in previous parishes where the help were paid so little they could hardly survive. At one assignment, the housekeeper had had three serious heart attacks. I asked her one day why she did not retire and rest. I was shocked when she said she could not afford to retire, as her salary was so little, her social security would be minimal. Also since her salary was so small she was unable to save anything; if she retired she could not survive. I had a very unpleasant scene with the pastor after that and he never got over it. Neither did I, so now I was determined to make sure that the people working for Mount Carmel were well compensated. I made sure their salaries were more than adequate, especially for the Office on Aging employees, thanks to federal and state contributions. The secretary and maintenance man were reasonably compensated. At the time, the State's power companies were having problems with their nuclear operations, and the price of their stocks dropped so low that the dividends they were paying came to 14%. I took the Perpetual Care Fund for the cemetery, which was receiving only 3% interest in the bank and bought I don't remember how many thousands of shares of New York State Gas and Electric stock. The dividends went far in helping pay Tony's salary, for the time he spent working on the cemetery grounds. Unfortunately, a year later the diocese told me to turn over the cemetery funds so they could be incorporated into one fund for all the cemeteries in the diocese, and said they would pay the parish, I think it was 4% interest. That was a real downer.

One important consideration in setting up the compensation package for parish workers was a reasonable pension plan. Since my unpleasant experience in previous parishes where the employees had no pension, I was determined to have a reasonable pension plan. One of the men on the parish council worked for Metropolitan Life. I asked him if he would look into their plans, and specifically a plan that was based on $1500 a year as a premium, as that was what the parish was paying the diocese for the parish workers' pension plan. He had the information in a matter of a week. Metropolitan's plan would pay our retired workers a guaranteed income of $1600 a month, but based upon recent payouts, it could be as high as $2000 a month.

With that documented information, I decided to see if our diocesan plan was better. We were already paying $1500 a year for the diocesan pension plan. I called to ask what the details of that plan were. The lady in charge did not know, but said the Prudential representative would be in the following Tuesday, and I could call and talk to him. The following Tuesday I called, and talked to the Prudential representative. He told me that, in the diocesan plan, when our employees retired at sixty-five they would receive about $250 a month. I told him that I had quote from Metropolitan Life and they offered a guaranteed $1600, but possibly as much as $2000 a month. The Prudential agent said, "Well, you can't beat that."

To give the diocese the benefit of my doubts, I assumed that the reason the payouts were so small was because the plan had only recently been put into operation and the diocese was trying to make up for the past by giving a little something to everyone who had been working for years with no pension. My bottom line was, whatever problems the diocese had, I felt in conscience I was responsible for those who were working with me, so I pulled out of the diocesan plan and, with the parish employees' consent, and the consent of the parish council, I signed on with Metropolitan Life's plan. I know I put the diocesan officials in a difficult position. It was not in good taste for a subordinate to go against diocesan policy and act independently, but I felt when a bishop put a priest in a position, he gave him the responsibility to care for a flock, and with that came the responsibility to do it conscientiously. That was one of the things I was terrified about when the idea of being pastor was first presented to me. It was very painful making this decision, but I had to do what I thought was right, even though no one could possibly understand me, and made me look like I was rebellious, and was determined to do things just my way. I hated being in this position, because my personality was such that I always wanted to please.

Two weeks later I got a letter from the insurance agency working for the diocese, telling me that it was impossible for Metropolitan to offer that much in pension payouts. Not knowing who was right, I sent to Metropolitan the letter I received from the diocese' agency. A week later I received a copy of a letter that Metropolitan had sent to the diocese' insurance agency, threatening a libel suit if they did not retract what they had written in their letter to me. With that forthcoming, the matter was settled as far as I was concerned, though it did not enhance my reputation with the chancery office.

The Office on Aging was now well on its way to serving the elderly, not just in the parish, but throughout the whole of Montgomery County, which, because it was mostly rural, was huge in size but small in population. The funding for the whole operation came not from the parish, but from donations from outside sources. So, although the parish was in charge of a vast operation, the parish itself was still struggling and needed constant attention to keep it ahead financially. This Office on Aging was a beautiful corporal works of mercy ministry for any parish, but for a small and poor parish like Mount Carmel it was a remarkable ecumenical advance, because there were not only Catholics, but Jewish people and people of various Protestant denominations, as well as others, involved in this community wide venture. It was the yeast in the dough working the way Jesus intended.

The people were happy with the various funds because they brought income from outside the parish, and as there were funerals practically every week, the outside income in lieu of flowers and Masses was steady and considerable. There was a fund for the poor, a fund to help kids getting out of jail, a fund for the elderly, a bell tower fund, a fund to maintain the grounds, and other funds which I have long forgotten.

Chapter Four

Now that the Office on Aging was running smoothly under the direction of its efficient director, with the generous help of Eileen Broyles, Brad's wife, the agency could now expand its programs. As one of the first ones to volunteer, Eileen contributed immensely from the start. Gilda Libertucci took care of the financial records and did a magnificent job. The caring work of the agency was drawing volunteers from the neighborhood and even from across the river, to help in much of the day to day work, so I could now finally concentrate on the parish.

We had the pipe organ construction completed, but we now needed a professional to play it. Going salaries were far beyond our means, and for a while we depended on generous volunteers. One of the volunteers was Mrs. Barbara De Rose. She was an excellent organist. We also needed a choir, which was no trouble organizing, as Italians love to sing, whether they can sing or not. This crowd could sing and were good at it, but none played the organ. However, I did get an idea. Italians, as well as others, like to light candles. We were using hundreds of vigil lights in the church. I checked to see what we were paying for them. I could not believe how much. I checked with Mobil at their main office at the Port of Albany, and found I could get the paraffin for twenty-five cents a pound. We needed a chemical material to retard burning and prevent excessive smoke. If we used that and made our own vigil lights we could have a profit of almost a dollar on each candle, which was much less than a pound. Besides supplying the needs of our own parish, I talked to the Jesuits at the shrine of the Jesuit and Indian Martyrs at Auriesville, and they agreed to use our candles. That was really worthwhile. So, now for an organist! I found that one of the mechanics at the local body shop was an accomplished organist. I invited him up to the parish and introduced him to the organ in church. He was thrilled, and asked if he could play it.

"Sure, I'd be delighted to hear it. I've been hoping I could find someone who could play the thing on a permanent basis."

He walked up to the organ console. I watched him. His pants were black with oil and grease stains, his hands were grease stained, his fingernails grimy. But, as soon as his greasy fingers touched that keyboard, it was as if an angel had come down from heaven. He started out with a Bach prelude and fugue, and then played Telemann and Hummel, all from memory, and flawless, and with deep feeling. When he finished, I asked him if he liked it.

"I love it. I would love to play it. Do you need an organist?"

"I do, but you'll have to earn your own salary as the parish is not as well off as your Lithuanian parish."

"How do I earn my salary?"

"Well, if you don't mind roughing it, and if you are willing to make the vigil lights for us, there will be enough income to pay you a good salary."

"How much?" This fellow was all business.

When I told him how much, he was delighted. So, now we had an organist, and a choir was beginning to take shape. Within a few weeks we had close to 35 members, making up in volume and enthusiasm what they lacked in polish. It would take time and effort to bring them to real quality. I wanted the choir up in the sanctuary and behind the altar, where they could be more in touch with the congregation. The organ console was off to the side of the sanctuary, so the choir and the congregation could easily work together, as it should be. In time, the choir surprised me when they all came to practice one night with beautiful blue and gold choir robes which they had made themselves.

I was shocked and asked them where they got those beautiful robes. They told me, that some of the women worked at Joel and Florence Kaplan's fabric factory and Joel gave them the material and let them make the robes on his machines. The Kaplans belonged to Rabbi Bloom's congregation and have always been dear friends. Unfortunately, I have lost track of them over the years as we are all 35 years older now, though I still have fond memories of those beautiful people.

With the choir's new choir robes, the sanctuary now looked complete. I designed an extension of the sanctuary floor, and Tony

Simiele worked with some of the parishioners in shaping the curve projecting out into where the first row of pews had been until we moved them up to the sanctuary as seating for the choir. The floor of the sanctuary and the steps down to the congregation level were then covered with a gorgeous red carpet donated by the one remaining carpet mill.

The choir met every Tuesday night and I soon found that even though they were volunteers, there was a price I had to pay. These were rough and ready guys who joined, and I had to have a bottle of brandy in the back room so some of the men's voices would still be in good shape for the second part of the rehearsal after the break. They told me, "What do you think, Father? We work hard all day and we have to keep our throats from getting dry." The women were much more accommodating. The men were a motley crew. Some were heavy equipment operators and ran D6 and D8 bulldozers all day long and by choir time their throats were dry with dust. Herm Iannotti had his own small print shop. Others had their gas station jobs, or were auto mechanics who worked since early morning. Some worked on city and county public work crews. One owned a high-quality, cabinet-making business and often hired troubled kids recently released from jail and was like a father to them, trying to get them to straighten out their lives. The interesting thing was that most of the choir members, even the men, didn't drink. They were just testing me, and the bottle of brandy was still half full two months later.

As it was always hard finding tenors, I soon realized the only way I could get them was if I trapped them. When people came up to the altar for Communion, I would say the words, "The Body of Christ," and the people would respond, "Amen," most of the time in an ordinary voice. Every now and then a man would respond in a high-pitched voice, and I knew I had a tenor. So, I put my hand on his shoulder and said, "Ah, you're a tenor. We need tenors, I want to see you after Mass." I know I should not have done that, but what could I do? It was the only way I could find tenors. At the next choir rehearsal, as soon as he walked in, everybody looked at him and laughed. These people all knew each other. He blushed, and with a broad grin, said, "I knew I shouldn't have gone to Communion Sunday. I heard about how he shanghaied tenors."

That choir was the source of so much joy and fun times for the parish. You really have to experience life in an Italian parish. The people are easily excitable, but they are full of joy and love of life, and in spite of difficult times, will always see the silver lining in times of the darkest clouds, and they are so appreciative of the smallest tokens of kindness to them. The parish family of Mount Carmel was that way. There was always some fun activity going on, and most everyone took part in it. And they could never do enough to help me. We had all bonded in a beautiful relationship, the way a parish should be. They loved the changes in the church and asked if I was going to do anything else. I told them I would really like to make the Blessed Sacrament chapel something very special. The tabernacle is just sitting there in an empty room with nothing inspiring about it. I would like to make it a very beautiful little chapel, and a quiet, sacred place where people can come and pray and feel close to Jesus.

One of the men in the parish who owned the cabinet making business, and did beautiful work, was always willing to help when I needed him. His name was Jimmy Di Caterino. I designed a tabernacle for the Blessed Sacrament. It was about two feet wide and a foot and half high. The roof was curved from front to around the back, with scalloped shingles covered with gold leaf. When he finished it, I painted it Wedgwood blue, with two doors in the front with blue background but each having an embossed angel facing each other, and painted white. Another friend was a glassblowing expert from GE and he offered to make a gorgeous, delicate glass shrine, with very complex glass designs enshrining the tabernacle, and measuring about two feet on either side of the tabernacle and curved over the top of the tabernacle. It took him about six months to finish the whole design. Jimmy finished his masterpiece in about two weeks. The other genius took much longer, but when he finished, it was stunning. At least we now had a beautiful tabernacle in place of the old one, and in a beautiful setting. The Blessed Sacrament chapel was a quiet, peaceful place for people to pray.

There were two stained glass windows on the outside wall facing the parking lot off the highway. On each side and between the two windows were large wall spaces about eight feet high and eight feet wide. I thought nice paintings of the Israelites harvesting the manna in the desert at early morning after sunrise would be nice, and another painting on that same wall but closer to the back wall where the tabernacle was located. This painting would depict the multiplication of the loaves and fishes with people in colorful dress sitting, as it says in the gospel story, in groups of 50 and a 100, and looking like flower gardens.

Fortunately, there was a very talented artist who was working in the ceramic operation. He was a genius, not only in painting, but in the making of ceramic molds and stained glass. He had at one time worked for a man who paid him only a few dollars an hour and kept him in the attic of his warehouse to work so nobody would get to know him. Bob made reproductions of Tiffany lampshades which the owner would sell out of town for $30,000 - $40,000 each, as Bob related to me.

This man and his wife became friends and joined the crew in our ceramic shop. His name was Bob Webster. His wife's name was Rita. I asked him if he would help me paint murals on the walls in the chapel. He was thrilled. So, a few days later, we started. We worked nights, and after he went home at about ten o'clock each evening, I continued painting until one or two o'clock in the morning. We continued this work for the next two or three months, when we finally finished. The only two things left were for me to put four beautiful hanging lamps in the ceiling, so people could read their missals and prayer books at Mass each morning, and to lay a beautiful light blue wall-to-wall Persian rug over the drab asphalt tile floor. With that done, I could relax.

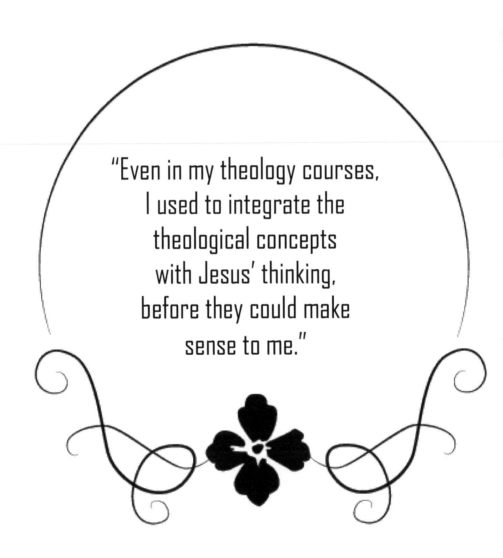

"Even in my theology courses,
I used to integrate the
theological concepts
with Jesus' thinking,
before they could make
sense to me."

Chapter Five

Not long after the pipe organ was installed and we had managed to hire an organist, I got a phone call from the chancery. The vice-chancellor was coming to talk with me. With him would be other officials, including the comptroller of the diocese, other chancery officials, as well as the diocesan superintendent of schools. They arrived after lunch the following day. When they arrived, they brought with them all kinds of accounting documents, including our parish financial reports to the diocese.

I knew what the meeting was going to be about, and the issues they would bring up, and I couldn't blame them. I knew I had made things very difficult for them, though I was not trying to be difficult, but there was no alternative to the way I had been running the parish and no other options to bring about a viable functioning community of caring people. I knew from the start that I was not going to make a good pastor in their eyes, but my being pastor was their idea, not mine. What was about to happen I could understand, but the parish did not have the financial means to do what they demanded.

The first question was about parish finances. I asked if I could go over to the office and get my own parish financial records, since the comptroller had the parish records on his lap. The vice-chancellor, Father Howard Russell, was always a decent gentlemanly priest whom I have always admired. He just listened.

The comptroller told me I did not need any books as I was a financial genius and knew about every penny that was in the records. And it was true, not that I was a genius, but that I knew of every penny that went in and out of all the various accounts. I always made sure that the records were kept in perfect order according to diocesan regulations, and I had total confidence in Gilda who was always so honest and meticulous in the way she kept the books. I was so fortunate to have a person like her who could give me the secure assurance that the records were always in keeping with diocesan regulations, and totally accurate.

The comptroller then proceeded to ask me where the $48,000 came from for the pipe organ. I told him that it was from a special fund that a parishioner started when his mother died, and from contributions pouring into that fund at the time of her funeral and afterwards, most of which came from people outside the parish.

"But, according to your records, the $48,000 was paid from your general parish account, which proves you used parish money to pay for the pipe organ. You told us once before that your parish was poor and that the total yearly income was only $25,000."

"I did not use parish money. Your own regulations specify that all moneys spent in the parish were to be channeled through the general checking account. And this should be done even if the funds for an individual expense were from another fund or account other than the general parish account. When an expense was to be made from that fund, your regulations direct that the money should be transferred from that fund into the general account, and the expense paid from the general account. So, if you check your records you will see that a withdrawal was made from the Pipe Organ Fund Savings Account and deposited the same day into the general parish account in keeping with your regulations. The check to pay for the pipe organ was then written from the general parish account, as you directed it should be. You should be more familiar with your own regulations."

He checked that information and said nothing. In the silence, the superintendent spoke up and asked about the $25,000 check I was supposed to send to the diocesan school office. I said that "the parish does not have that kind of money, and there is no way I can come up with it. The parishioners are very poor here, and I don't have the heart, knowing especially how they feel about how you people have treated them in the past, to even consider trying to raise that kind of money from them."

"But, you have money for all kinds of other things. Where do you get all that money?"

"I intentionally send down to the chancery every week my parish bulletin, explaining honestly everything I do here in the parish. Everything is an open book, and I keep nothing hidden from you. If you had read the bulletins, you would know everything about the parish, and every little thing I do here. I cannot understand why you question me like this."

The comptroller then asked me why I have all these various funds. "We have these funds because I and the parish council thought it would be a good idea if we asked people to make donations to different causes in lieu of flowers and donations for Masses on the occasion of deaths in the parish, which is practically every week or two. In the past, there were so many Masses requested that it would take over three years to catch up. I thought that was ridiculous, as it made it impossible to offer a Mass when someone was ill or wanted a Mass offered for someone's birthday, or just for some live person, or just to offer a Mass to thank God for his goodness to all of us. I think it's morbid to be offering Masses just for dead people, most of whom were probably already in heaven. There are many other reasons why people would like to have Mass offered. These funds make that possible, and also help the parish to draw in money from outside the parish so we can do more things for the parish which our limited parish donations would never permit."

There were other things discussed, all centering around the same issues. It was not a pleasant meeting. I knew deep down they did not trust me, and did not realize how honest I was being with them. I could not help but wonder what the previous pastor told the chancery about the financial condition of the parish, as these officials seemed to think I did have adequate funds to give them what they demanded. When the vice-chancellor finally ended the meeting, he said he would like to see the new pipe organ, and told the other officials he wanted them to see it as well. The vice-chancellor was a pianist himself and had been encouraging parishes to have pipe organs.

We all then went over to the church. It just happened that the organist was on a late lunch break from the auto body shop where he worked, and, as a regular part of his schedule, would come up, with soiled work clothes and grease-stained hands to practice on the organ, which he happened to be doing at the time. So, the group, following the vice-chancellor's instructions, all sat in the first pew listening to a remarkable display of classical organ pieces which the organist did without one piece of music in front of him. They had to be impressed but walked out afterwards saying nothing, except for the chancellor, who came over to me and said, "Joe, I want to apologize for the way we have been treating you since you came here. Seeing the parish and all the things that are going on here, this is the way every parish should be run."

How healing those words were to me! But, it was only a short time later that that kind priest had not only left the chancery, but left the priesthood. A week or so later, Gilda, our parish secretary-treasurer received a letter from the diocesan finance people saying they wanted a financial statement every three months. A short time later, it was changed to every month. For all other parishes in the diocese it was only every six months. Besides that, I found out from a well-placed friend that the business office had been contacting all the local banks in the capital district to see if I had any hidden accounts. This total lack of trust was painful, but it wasn't just a lack of trust.   What hurt is that they really were convinced that I was devious and dishonest.

Strangely enough, I could understand how the officials felt and I could not blame them for their reactions to me. But, I had a job to do to be a good shepherd to my parishioners, even if my own superiors were my most serious hindrance. I still could ill afford to let the situation bother me, though when I went back into the rectory when the officials left, the cook was in the kitchen crying. She had been working in the kitchen, during the meeting and had heard everything. I told her that it was all right, they were just upset because of the way I do things. "But, doesn't it bother you?" she asked. "No, Lena. I was shocked but, it doesn't bother me. Lena, I have gone through so much in my life as a priest, I now become like a piece of cold steel when I have a job to do. I can't let anything distract me from what I have to do, so don't let what happened upset you. I'm all right." I gave her a hug and told her I was glad she was such a help to me.

Work in the parish was moving smoothly. At our parish council meetings I had told the members that I had learned to trust them, and would like to share important responsibilities with them. I told them, "This is **your** parish. Pastors come and go. You people know how to take care of your families. Some of you have your own businesses and you know how to run them. There is no reason why you cannot run the parish. It is not that complicated. Besides, difficult times are ahead for the Church, and the time will come when you won't have a priest, and then you will have to run your parish. So, I would like to start now. We can work together, so you will be well prepared for the time when a shortage of priests will be critical. What I would like to do is set up a number of committees to cover all the important areas of parish life. I will appoint the chair-persons because I don't want any politicking going on. We can ask parishioners to choose whatever committee they would like to serve on. The committees will then meet, not up here at the church, but at your homes. That's where the parish is. These are just buildings here. Parish life is out there in your community. You are to be the leaven in that larger community, causing it to rise to a higher level. I will not attend any of your meetings, though the day after you meet, I would like the chairperson of the meeting to come to the rectory and share with me what was discussed and what was decided. I will respect your decisions, and though I might offer some advice, I will let you make your own mistakes, and work them out."

"What do you mean, shortage of priests?" one person asked.

"You have to believe me. There will be a severe shortage, and many parishes will not have priests. The parishes who can take care of themselves will survive."

"You think we can do it, Father?"

"I know you can. It is not that complicated."

They agreed to try it. I suggested a number of committees which I felt they should consider: the finance committee, the grounds committee, a committee for the religious instruction of the young people, a liturgy committee, a committee to work with the poor, a cemetery committee, a committee to work with the young people being released from jail, a committee to work with the elderly, a committee to work with the Jewish people as needed, a committee to work with the Protestant people, which at that point was the Lutheran Pastor Don Marxhausen and his people, with whom we already had joint programs. There were other committees which I cannot remember.

Although I had turned over practically all my authority to the parishioners, I had more authority than any dictatorial pastor, as the people were so appreciative of my trust in them, that they made sure they would not decide anything that they knew would be offensive to me, and they always felt comfortable coming and asking for my suggestions. I had become, for all practical purposes, their teacher and spiritual leader, which I always thought was what priests should be anyway.

I must admit; I was not disappointed. They had their meetings. They made very prudent decisions. Knowing there was very little money available, they made decisions that reached out to people and accomplished many worthwhile goals in the community that needed expenditure of energy and good will, with hardly any expenditure of parish funds. By that time, we were well into our third year in the parish, and I cannot tell you what a joy it was working with these people. It was hard to believe what wonderful dreams they had of what Church could be like.

The relationship with the Jewish people was particularly warm. Rabbi Bloom's wife took part in the ceramic classes. A Jewish lawyer volunteered to serve as legal consultant to our Office on Aging, and provided valuable help to many senior citizens. Other Jewish people offered help in whatever way they could. A toy store owner, Emmanuel Rosen, knew that on Christmas Eve, we had a horse and sleigh with Santa Claus that went through the whole South Side neighborhood. Lena, my cook, had made a gigantic bag, and long before Christmas, went down to the toy store to buy enough toys for the children in our parish neighborhood. I am sure Emmanuel lost money on the deal as he was so generous to us. Then, on Christmas Eve, Santa Claus drove his sleigh down through the parish passing out Christmas presents to all the children as they gathered along the street singing Christmas carols, excited about seeing a real Santa Claus coming down the street with a huge bag of toys for everybody. I don't know who got the most fun out of the event, the children or the grandparents who were standing there with them as the parents were home, preparing their traditional Italian fish smorgasbord for later.

As time went on other beautiful things took place throughout the community as the people had become the yeast in the dough, causing the spiritual level, as well as the social level, to rise to a new and exciting level. And the wonderful thing about it was, I could take no credit whatsoever. It was all done by these unsophisticated people's remarkable understanding of what it meant to be "church."

Our relationship with Pastor Marxhausen's Lutheran parish was a remarkable expression of ecumenism. We had become very good friends. He once invited me to be part of a ceremony on Reformation Sunday in his parish. He wanted to re-enact the excommunication of Martin Luther. I vested as a priest up in his pulpit while he stood in with his congregation. And at the proper time. I read the solemn excommunication before his entire congregation. It was very dramatic. I had been reluctant to do it, but decided I would go ahead with it, because then he would owe me one, which chip I cashed in shortly thereafter. It was during July when our parish was preparing for the Feast of Our Lady of Mount Carmel. A solemn, nine-day novena was customary in the parish in preparation for this feast. Long standing traditions in the Carmelite Order to which I once belonged and which is dedicated to Our Lady of Mount Carmel, tell of Jesus and his mother visiting the ancient Jewish hermits living on Mount Carmel at the time of Jesus, and since that time had become Jesus' disciples. So, when we prepared for the celebration of the feast, it centered on Mary as the Mother of the Messiah.

Knowing that Martin Luther always had a deep and warm devotion to Mary, which most Lutherans are not aware of, I decided to ask my Lutheran friend if he would like to give one of the sermons in preparation for the coming feast of our parish. "Girzone, you are pushing my ecumenism way too far. You know we Lutherans don't go that Mary route."

"Strange," I said, "then, you're not a very good Lutheran because your founder had a wonderful devotion to the Blessed Mother, and he used to give beautiful sermons on Mary. Too bad you people didn't follow him in that."

I knew I was pushing him way past his limits, but he said he would think it over. That night, or rather the next morning at about two o'clock, I got a phone call. I was in a deep sleep. It was the "German Shepherd."

"Hello," I said in a gravelly voice.

"Damn you, Girzone, I can't sleep and you're not going to sleep either."

"What's bothering you, big bear, which is what I used to call him when he was in an ugly mood, at other times it was usually 'my favorite German shepherd?'"

"I've just spent the last three hours reading Luther's sermons on Mary."

"It's about time."

"Don't push me, Girzone."

I just laughed, and said, "Well, what's next?"

"Yeah, I'd be happy to do a sermon on Mary, but it's going to be one of Luther's sermons, not mine."

"Great, I'd rather have his than yours anyway."

"At least I prepare mine," was his parting shot, knowing that I never prepared my sermons, because of an agreement I made with God, that I would let him speak to the people through me.

After wishing each other a good night's sleep, we both hung up.

The novena was a special event in the parish. The night Pastor Marxhausen came with his parishioners was very special for all of us. It was probably the first time his people had heard a sermon on Mary, and by Martin Luther, and it certainly was the first time our people heard a sermon by Martin Luther. All of us were deeply inspired, because it was a beautiful sermon. I don't know whether it was that night or another night that we worshipped together. We tried to do it in a liturgically proper way. We both shared the altar. He had bread and wine on his half of the altar and I had bread and wine on my half of the altar. We said the prayers together, each of us consecrating our own bread and wine, and then later distributing Communion to our own people. It was clearly explained to the people beforehand so there would be no misunderstanding. We all felt afterwards it was one of the most beautiful religious experiences we all had, and was a giant move forward in our progress toward our two parishes considering merging, which unfortunately, did not take place as Pastor Marxhausen's wife divorced him, and it had a profound effect on his life, which, however, brought us closer together as friends as it was a real crisis time for him. Only one thing we still wanted to do for both of our parishes while there was still time, was for our two bishops to co-confirm the children in both our parishes. In spite of my problems with the chancery staff, the bishop was gracious enough to agree to it, as was the Lutheran bishop. Unfortunately, before we could make arrangements for the ceremony, Pastor Marxhausen took an assignment to a parish outside Chicago.

I think it must have been around that time that I was beginning to feel weak, and noticed I was having pains in my chest. I thought nothing of it as I was always strong and healthy. I slept well, and I ate well and I used up plenty of energy each day. I got my exercise by working on chores around the parish. The entrance to the parish grounds from Route 5W was dangerous because it was narrow and there were ditches on each side of the entrance. I decided it would be good exercise for me to build a wall on each side of the driveway. Unfortunately, there was not enough soil to dig three feet for a footing to prevent heaving from the frozen ground, so in place of a footing, I pounded a good number of three quarter inch reinforcement rods almost three feet into the ground and then built the two stonewalls around the extended upper sections of the rods. Now after over 30 years the walls still have no cracks, even though they are resting on top of the ground, with reinforcement rods as the only footing.

I think that the work that I had done may have been a little too much, though emotional stress played a part, I am sure, but I was beginning to feel weak and different in a way I could not understand. It was a Friday afternoon while driving through the city, and I had horrible pains in my chest. I was not far from the hospital, so I thought it might be a good idea to stop in and be checked. I went into the emergency ward; the doctor examined me and said everything seemed to be okay, but he wanted to keep me there for a few days for observation. I said, "I appreciate your checking, doctor, but I won't be able to stay. There are no priests to cover my parish for weekend Masses. I'll have to leave, but if you want me to, I will come back Monday."

The doctor was stunned. "I can't release you. It would be irresponsible. You will have to sign yourself out." I did, and went right back to the rectory and rested. I did feel weak. I had no trouble all weekend, and was able to offer my Masses, and do whatever else was expected. On Monday morning, I went out to my vegetable garden on the opposite side of the church near the highway. While I was working in the garden, I had that terrible pain again, and fell down on the blacktop. There was no one around, and I did not know what to do. I rested for a few minutes, hoping the pain would go away, but it didn't. I decided I had better work my way over to the rectory on the other side of the church, and ask Lena if she would drive me to the hospital. I could trust her not to panic. She always had a cool head whenever there was a crisis. I guess it was her tough Sicilian heritage that kept her cool in difficult times. I mentioned that to her on the way over to the hospital. She laughed and told me a story of how one day her car stalled as she was crossing a railroad. She could not get it started. So, after hearing the train in the distance she ran way up the tracks and frantically waved to the engineer to stop, screaming out to him that her car was stuck on the track. Fortunately, it was a freight train and was not going at high speed. He stopped in time and got out and helped her get the car started, and a big crisis was avoided.

"Lena, I'm glad you work for the parish, no wonder you don't let things around the parish bother you."

"You have to remember, Father, I grew up with all these people, and by now we're used to each other, that's why I can give you good advice about each one, and who to be careful of. Everybody's related in some way, and I try to help you avoid creating any unnecessary crises."

By that time, we were at the hospital. The doctor was glad to see I was still alive and this time he had no trouble admitting me. I was in the hospital for the next four or five days for observation. There was evidence that I did have a heart attack, but there was no permanent damage. He told me I was going to have angina pains frequently and that I should take the nitroglycerin tablets which he was prescribing for whenever I got those pains. He also put me on a strict diet which I scrupulously kept. I did have serious angina pains for the next year, but by carefully following the doctor's instructions concerning the medicine and the diet, after

69

that year I never had a heart pain again. That was over 30 years ago.

About this time, after my experiences with Don Marxhausen, and other clergy, who could not understand why I was so Jesus oriented, I began to realize that Jesus and his priorities as the Good Shepherd, were not high priorities even with clergy. I expected the chancery officials to understand what I was doing and why, and I began to realize how far apart were our values and vision. For the first time I was beginning to have feelings that I should write a book about Jesus, since he seemed to be far removed from religious people's consideration in decision-making. They may talk about him, and say we have to be like Jesus, but, I was finding out that few people even know much about Jesus. In studying the phenomenon, I was beginning to realize that Jesus has been pushed very much into the background of Christian churches. He is no longer the focus of religion as he was for the first 1500 years of Christianity. He has been supplanted by catechisms, and the memorizing of doctrines that define our denominational beliefs and differences, and assure our separateness from one another as Christians.

This thought struck me that Jesus had become the lost Treasure in Christianity, and that clergy knew very little about Jesus because he was not taught in seminaries, either Catholic or Protestant. Although priests and ministers could quote chapter and verse, and comment superficially on gospel stories, that was not the same as talking in depth about the person we were supposed to have dedicated our lives to understand and follow. Making Jesus come alive for people was critical, but few could do it. The many clergy who were not kind to people reminded me of callous Pharisees and scribes. And I could see how these good people at Mount Carmel could make their parish come alive and reflect so beautifully what Jesus had originally intended for his Church. They made the gospels come to life, and were having a revitalizing effect on the whole Amsterdam community, and other communities around as well.

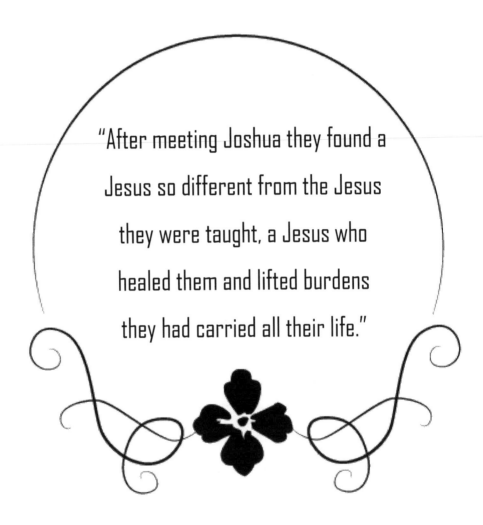

"After meeting Joshua they found a Jesus so different from the Jesus they were taught, a Jesus who healed them and lifted burdens they had carried all their life."

Chapter Six

The parish was running smoothly under the care of the parishioners. They had their dreams of what their parish could be like and the effect they would like the parish to have not just on parish life, but on the larger community. They had a new and healthy self-image, and were proud of their accomplishments and the parish's new image in the whole Amsterdam community.

My own responsibilities were greatly reduced, and I had more time to relax, which for me meant spending fun time planting flowering trees around the parish grounds, and up in the cemetery and painting pictures. Andy Gigliotti, my friend who made arrangements for the pipe organ, asked if I would paint a picture for him. Besides being a funeral director, he was a very discriminating collector of antiques and original paintings. He wanted a painting that was a combination of a Grandma Moses and a Currier and Ives. I set up the easel at the foot of my bed and when I was lying on the bed I would stare at the canvas and try to create the picture in my imagination. That was the only way I could paint. As soon as I had the whole picture in my mind, I could paint it in rapid time, though blending the sharp primitive colors of Grandma Moses and the soft antique mood of a Currier and Ives took considerable adjusting but it worked. The finished product was 36" by 48". Andy was happy with it. Many years later I tried to buy it back, but had no luck.

Around the same time an elderly man came up to the rectory and asked if I would paint a picture for his church. He had either a Polish, a Lithuanian, or Slovak accent, which was difficult to understand. I told him I did not think I was good enough an artist to do artwork for a church. He told me a priest had recommended that he come to me. After he left, I found a shopping bag at the back door. It contained three coffee cans full of silver quarters and half dollars. My first reaction was annoyance that the man was telling me he would not take no for an answer. My second reaction was guilt. I began to feel ashamed that I could at least have given his request a more courteous consideration, but as I did not know the man's name or how to contact him, the package of coins was a constant prick at my conscience. Then, every so often I would find another can of coins at the back door. Finally, my conscience couldn't take it any longer, so I decided I had to paint the picture for the man. I wanted the picture to have Jesus in a casual relaxed mood with Peter, just the two of them. The setting was in Jesus' favorite camping site when in Jerusalem, the Garden of Olives. Jesus and Peter were sitting with their backs against two ancient olive trees with their lunch and a flask of wine lying on a rock between them. One of Jesus' sandals was off to the side of his foot. In the distance was the walled city of Jerusalem, with the gold of the Temple shining brilliantly in the sun. The temple setting was strangely framed within an opening formed by two oddly growing branches. I always wanted to see a picture of Jesus just relaxing in some kind a peaceful setting. I could never find one. I thought

74

there might be others who would have the same feeling. It took me about six months of steady work to finish the painting and I just hoped the man would show up so I could give it to him.

One day, when I least expected, I saw him approaching the back door of the rectory. He looked frail and tired. I brought him inside and asked him how he was. "Not good, Father. Not good." That was all he said. He asked if I would please consider doing the painting for him. I told him I had a surprise for him. I went up to my bedroom, took the painting off the easel and brought it downstairs. When he saw it, he beamed and his face became radiant, and all he said was, "Thank you, thank you so much, Father." I didn't ask him if he liked it. I could tell by his reaction. Then I went upstairs and brought down all the cans of coins he had left. When he saw them and realized I intended to give them back to him, he looked so hurt. "No, no, Father. I want you to have them. I am an old man. I have little time left and I have no need for them. Please don't refuse my little gift. That is all I have to thank you." The man's humility and frailty brought tears to my eyes. The man told me where I could drop off the painting and he would pick it up at that spot immediately if I would tell him when I would bring it there. I told him the time I would drop it off, and I did bring it there at precisely that time. I thought perhaps he was homeless, and was ashamed to tell me. I still knew nothing about him, not his name, nor where he lived nor what happened to him, until a short time later, when the parish organist told me that he had just played the organ at the funeral of an old man for whom I had painted a picture a short time ago for his church. I cannot think of the beauty of that simple man's soul and the profound effect his strange appearances and disappearances had on me. To this day I cannot recall that memory without tears.

For some reason or other old people seemed to just appear at my back door. Sometimes I think it was just from loneliness. Every Sunday morning, an old timer by the name of Tony, would be sitting at the back door of the rectory waiting for me to go over to the eight o'clock Mass. It was when we had changed the Mass schedule after Father Patterson was reassigned.

Tony was well into his eighties, maybe even older. His wife had died during the past year, and he spent much of his time working in his garden and inviting his friends over to play cards and drink his homemade wine, which was quite good. One Sunday morning as he accompanied me over to the church, I asked him if he was missing his wife a lot.

"Of course, padre. She was a good woman. I loved her very much, and miss her terribly."

I said to him, "Tony, I bet you can't wait for God to take you home, so you can be with your wife."

"No, no, padre, don't talk like that."

"Why, Tony?"

"Because I know what I got here, but I don't know what I'm going to get over there."

Every now and then Tony would bring me vegetables from his garden and a bottle of his homemade wine and we would sit and talk and sip wine, while nibbling on Italian cookies.

I had fun with the old timers, which was most of the parish. I knew they liked dandelions, and so did I. So, when spring came each year, I would put a note in the parish bulletin telling them that I would not have the lawn cut in the field behind the school until the men had finished picking their dandelions. They got a laugh out of that, just thinking that I would hold off on the mowing until they got their dandelions. They appreciated it and when they finished, they always brought me some, too. We also had a lot of fun each spring over who would win the pool for having the first homegrown tomato of the season and who would have the biggest tomato by the end of the growing season. One day I got a sad phone call from a dear friend, Sisto Vigliotti, who was probably the best backyard farmer in the parish. He would have won, but when he woke up this particular morning he had to call first thing to tell me a mouse had eaten all his tomato seedlings. His friends were delighted because now they all had a chance to win.

On an occasional Saturday morning, especially in the bitter cold winters, I would cook pancakes and sausages for a group of men who were all loyal helpers, most of whom usually hung around Moe Sandy's gas station. There was Moe Sandy, Herm Iannotti, John Chirico, Pat Zumbolo, Freddie Sandy, George Sandy, Jimmy Di Caterino, Joe Langley, Joe O'Shea, and whoever else happened to show up. These were some of the happiest times in the parish. These men had grown up together, knew each other and never let die the childhood memories of crazy and embarrassing things each of them did in times past. I had never been with a noisier crowd. Their wives were very special women, and were much more refined than the men. But, all these families, and the way they behaved with each other, for some reason, made scenes in the gospel become real for me. The group on Saturday mornings reminded me of the time when Levi, the tax collector, threw a big party for Jesus, and the house was filled with Levi's noisy colleagues, much to the shock of the Pharisees who were walking down the street. The only thing that was different was that most of my men didn't drink alcohol, especially Moe Sandy.

On one particular Saturday morning, however, Moe had a bad chest cold. I could tell it was on the verge of becoming pneumonia. All he wanted to drink was hot tea. I wish I had had some grappa, but I didn't. I said, "Tea? Moe, let me give you something that will knock that cold out of your chest. Just trust me, Moe."

"I did once before, but I'll give you this one chance."

I made a nice tea drink. It was hot and had a very nice flavor.

"Well, I have to admit it tastes good," he said. "I could get attached to this. It tastes sort of like orange."

When the party ended and we put all the dishes in the kitchen, and went outside as the men got into their cars and trucks to leave, poor Lena finally emerged from nowhere to clean up the mess we had all made. She didn't mind. She knew all these guys and they were her favorite people. I did help her a bit, but she said she could do a better job if she did it by herself.

About an hour later, I got a telephone call from Moe Sandy's gas station. The men were still hanging around down there. Herm Iannotti said I'd better get down there right away. I jumped in my car and drove down to the gas station. The guys were all sitting around the pot belly stove. It looked like a scene from one of Norman Rockwell's paintings.

Moe looked strangely relaxed. "Moe, are you all right?" I asked, concerned. I sensed that was the reason why they called me down there. "Yeah, I'm in great shape. Cough is gone, feel great, but when I try to pump gas I can't find the opening for the gas tank. What did you put in that drink?"

"You said it was good."

"It was good all right, but I can't get my work done."

"But, look all the help you got here, all your friends."

"They're no help. They just come in here to keep warm. They would rather sit here and laugh at me."

"Moe," Pat Zumbolo shouted out, (he never talked in a low voice) "you have to admit, you are funny."

We all laughed, and I said, "Really, Moe, I put only a little Southern Comfort in your tea, but, I have to admit, it was 100 proof."

Next morning at Mass, I asked Moe about his cold.

"What cold? Are you kidding, no bug could have survived that drink."

These were some of the main characters in Joshua, though some of their last names may have been changed. Joshua's life was well centered around this crew, and a number of others who were also friends, like Woozie (Salvatore Dominick) and Tony Casapullo.

Chapter Seven

It was never dull in the parish. If there was not something going on in the parish, there were situations outside the parish that were brought to my back door. Being so active in the Schenectady community, people in neighboring communities were aware of my involvement because of the constant television and other media coverage. That was always a liability for me at each new assignment.

It wasn't very long after I became pastor at Our Lady of Mount Carmel that a man called and asked if he could talk with me. Shortly later he came to the rectory and told me his story. He was the building inspector for the city of Amsterdam, and poured his heart out over the very difficult time he was having enforcing the building code, especially since there were serious, life-threatening violations. When I asked him what kind of violations were involved, he told me that many of them were electrical violations. In many cases, the electric wires were just strung across rooms throughout the house rather than being contained inside the walls and properly channeled to the electrical panels. Also, a number of two and three story houses had no rear exits from the second and third stories, so if there was a fire, occupants had no means of escape, and could be seriously injured, or burnt alive. Such situations are forbidden by code. When I asked him why they were not enforced, his reply was, because the buildings were owned by city officials, one of them in the fire department. The houses were occupied by poor people.

"The reason I come to you, Father, is because if you work with me, I think we can get these violations cleared up."

I told the man I admired his courage, and promised to do what I could, but deep down, I wished that I could avoid this kind of involvement, as I always paid a high price for it. What I told him I could do was call my friends at the television channel who had been such a help to me in the past, and alert them to this situation.

The television people were concerned, as I knew they would be, and said they would come up and do a story on it, but asked me if I could accompany them, which was what I was hoping to avoid. However, since they felt it was important that I be involved if I wanted to make an impact on the community, I finally ended up going with the inspector and the television crew. That one episode accomplished what was intended, and there were no obvious, immediate, personal repercussions, but it lit a fuse that kept smoldering, and in time surfaced into a nasty situation.

At the same time, there were long-term problems in the parish that took me a while to become aware of, and that was gambling, and things associated with it. It was not only rampant in the neighborhood, but it was a big part of the parish celebrations. And it was not just ordinary gambling, but heavy gambling. When I realized how much money was involved and how deeply entrenched it was, and that it was endemic to the neighborhood itself, I was very disturbed. It was so much a part of life in the area that even the little kids grew up with it, so I made up my mind it was going to end. I did not want to involve the parish council because it would not have been fair. Many of their relatives and friends were involved, so I made the decision myself and banned all gambling in the parish. I even banned bingo, even though it meant losing half the annual income of the parish.

Interestingly, the people were understanding of my predicament and eventually agreed to eliminate the gambling at parish affairs, but the bingo became an issue. The elderly women in the parish, and in the neighborhood, called me and came up to talk to me. Their message was the same, "Father, how can you cut out our bingo? It the only time we get a chance to go out and spend time with our friends. So, we spend five dollars. That's not much for a night out, and we have a good time sitting with our friends and catching up with what happened during the week. That's our only recreation. Don't take away our bingo, Father."

As reluctant as I was, I had to let the bingo stay. I had never looked at bingo in that way before, and the women were right, what harm was there in it, and they weren't spending money needed for other things. It was their only night out, and a cheap night out at that, and the only time they had to spend time with their friends. They were stuck in the house all week long, and were not able to get around the way they used to, especially as many of them were widows.

Even though I got rid of the other gambling in the parish, there was still gambling throughout the community, where men would come together to play cards, or place bets. Everybody knew where these places were. In time, many of these gamblers became friends and started coming to church. I found out that these men were good contributors to the political campaigns even to the campaigns of candidates for Supreme Court. But, that was not a concern of mine. My concern was to get my sheep back into the flock, and worshipping with their families. In time, most of them did become active and enjoyed it.

Once I became active in the community at large, I knew other people would be asking for help. One was a Korean family, the Lims. They were the nicest people. Mrs. Lim was a concert pianist but found it difficult to find work in that field ever since she and her husband came to the States.

Mr. Lim was a karate instructor, an excellent one, and set up a karate class in one of our vacant classrooms. It was as a favor to me because I was trying to put the building to good use, to help defray expenses especially at that time when we were in the middle of the first energy crisis, and oil and electric costs began to skyrocket.

The family was a special kind of Catholic family, cultured, well-educated, very wholesome and deeply religious. Mr. Lim's brother was director of Catholic Charities in the Archdiocese of Seoul, South Korea, and his family in Korea was very involved with the Church.

When Mr. Lim came to the rectory, I could tell he had been crying. When I told him he looked very upset, he broke down and told me what had happened. He had been granted a valid visa years before, but suddenly an immigration judge decided arbitrarily that the visa was obtained fraudulently, and that the Lim's were given forty-eight hours to get all their belongings together and appear at the airport, to be shipped back to Korea. I used the word 'arbitrarily' because, when asked, the judge could not give an answer and said he did not have to give an answer, but that that was his decision. Mr. Lim already had his green work permit card and his social security, and all his papers were in order, but the judge's decision was final.

I had just baptized the Lim's new baby, who was only three months old by that time. They had two other children besides, one also a baby. I also knew what being deported entailed, and it was not by air flight, but by train and each night stopping at a different city, and sleeping in a jail cell, and the same every night until they finally reached the west coast. Mr. Lim was afraid that the little baby might not survive such conditions. He also said that he had a house for which he was making mortgage payments each month, and a car. There was no way he could make provisions to dispose of these things in two days. He asked if there was anything I could do. He was so distraught. He asked me if I thought God would forgive him, if he committed suicide so his wife could marry an American and stay in the country with the babies.

This was something entirely new for me. I did not know where even to begin. All we had was less than 48 hours. I told Mr. Lim to pray hard and not do anything stupid, and I would pray hard, too, and get in touch with him as soon as I had a plan. A plan, a plan, where was I going to get a plan? I prayed, and knew God would help. Out of nowhere, the thought came to me to call the Canadian embassy in New York City, which I did immediately. It was almost closing time, but the call made it through. The lady with whom I talked was most gracious. After explaining the situation as completely as I could, she told me to have Mr. and Mrs. Lim go to New York the next day and meet with her, and she would make her decision.

I called the Lims immediately, told them what to do, and then said, "Make sure you take your babies with you when you go to the embassy. This they did. I waited and prayed all the next day. Late the following day, on returning home, they called me and said that the officials at the Canadian embassy in New York made arrangements for them to go to Canada, and live there. They got together what belongings they could take and immediately took off for Canada, where they had no trouble crossing the borders with the papers they had been given. Fortunately, they were able to accomplish all this before the 48 hours were up. I breathed a deep sigh of relief and had never been so grateful to God, especially for such a quick answer to desperate prayers.

Then the real work started. I had to find a way to get them back into the country sometime in the future. For this, they needed Labor Department approval for a labor application. And for Labor Department approval, it had to be for work requiring specialized abilities to fill a position needed by an American-run business or program. Fortunately, at the time I had some dear friends, one of whom worked in the Labor Department, and was a friend of Governor Rockefeller. My friend's name was Nick Valentine. Nick was of Greek descent and politically shrewd. He was the Deputy Commissioner of Labor for the State of New York. We had become friends long before, because whenever he needed help he came to me, and whenever I needed help, I went to Nick, and we were always there for each other. His daughter Linda and I were also best of friends, as well his long-suffering wife Gen, who put up with us.

After telling Nick the whole situation, he immediately set up the strategy, telling me step-by-step what I had to do. The first thing was to go to the Albany immigration office and get an application and fill it out. This I did immediately. I brought the papers home, filled them out and went back down with the papers and gave them to the office person, and paid the fee. I waited for weeks and heard nothing. I went back down and they refused to see me. After my third visit, they finally told me it was rejected, and that I should apply again. But, they never told me what was needed. I did this I don't know how many times, and it kept being rejected. I got tired of paying the fees, so I called up Nick. He put me in touch with one of his assistants in the Brooklyn office. She sent me the precise application I needed and directed me step-by-step as to how I was to fill it out, which I did. So far the greater part of a year had passed.

During that time, I was continually checking up on the Lim family to see how they were surviving in Canada. They were doing fine. They had met with a large colony of Koreans living near Toronto, and Mr. Lim had started a business. "What kind of a business, Limmy?"

"Collecting worms."

"Collecting worms? What kind of a business is that?"

"It's a very good business. I have a truck. I have a hundred workers, and I have permission to go out to the golf courses at night and pick worms. My workers have head lamps, and crawl along the greens and the low-cut grass and pick worms as they come out at night. We collect tens of thousands of them every night, and I pay my workers well, and I do well."

"What do you do with the worms?" I asked him totally overwhelmed with curiosity.

"I sell them to the fishing industry in Boston and Cape Cod. So far I made $50,000."

I was absolutely flabbergasted. I had never known such industrious people in my whole life. I then told him I was making progress with his application, but that it was painfully slow, and a lot of things were happening in the parish and in town which demanded attention.

One of the nicest involvements was with Pastor Don Marxhausen. He and I had been discussing our different beliefs, and I thought it would be good if we could take the Nicene Creed, and teach it to our people in such a manner that we could profess it together in a way that was acceptable to both congregations.

"Girzone, don't do this to me. Don't expect me to accept the infallibility of the pope."

"Big Bear, I didn't say a thing about the infallibility of the pope."

"I know you, Girzone, especially after the job you did on me with Mary and Luther. I still get 'agida' when I think of it."

"Big Bear, but all I suggest is that we get down to basics. Either we are going to take Jesus seriously or our ecumenism is just talk and a farce. I have questions about personal infallibility, but I don't have a problem with the indefectibility of the Church, nor do I have a problem with the fact that Jesus gave Peter special authority, not as a personal gift, but as a responsibility he had to guide the whole Church and an authority and power that would be passed down to his successors to guarantee the faithful transmission of his teachings in their integrity until the end of time."

"I can believe that," he responded.

"So, what's your problem?"

"I still don't trust you, Girzone. If you expect to add that to the Nicene Creed, and have my people go along with it, you're out of your mind."

"Did I say that?"

"No, but I know how that mafia mind of yours works."

"All right, you believe it, I believe it. There must be some of your people who could understand it the way we do. That could be a basis if we explain it to them and to my people, too. I am willing to admit my limitations as to what I can accept, and you can, too. The issue is: are you a shepherd that leads the sheep or a shepherd that follows the sheep?"

"Now you're being a wise guy, Girzone."

"You have to admit; I did let you introduce my people to Martin Luther. How many other priests would have done that? I stuck my neck out. And I know you have too. You're about the only one I know who has the guts to take on difficult issues and are willing to pay the price for it. This is something that we both have wanted to do for a long time. Your time is short. Mine is too. Shall we take the bold leap?"

"Let me sleep on it, and struggle with my nightmares. My people are not as easygoing as your Italians. Germans are different; they can be tough. They have been good to me, but I can go only so far. I'll let you know."

It took a few weeks for Don, which was his real name, to get over his nightmares and we finally put a joint Eucharistic service together, with the same propriety as before, and made a profession of faith which included Jesus' words to Peter, not as a personal privilege but as guarantee of the faithful transmission of Jesus' teachings in their integrity until the end of time. It was difficult for both of us, but we felt we made a little step forward in helping our two peoples to understand each other and accept a belief that we could accept and profess together.

That liturgy was our last together and though we parted forever, we bonded through what we had accomplished through our people in a way that was to keep us forever close. Years later I called him and asked him about his son, Peter, whom I always said, might end up a pope someday. His comment was priceless. "He will make an interesting pope. Already as a teenager he is high on poverty and questionable on chastity." I know he was joking, but he just couldn't resist a chance to shock me.

The parish was still going under full steam. The bell tower fund had enough money to pay for the construction of the tower and order the carillon system. Woozie the welder, and a future character in Joshua, built the steel tube structure and charged only for material. Jerry Riggi was again approached, and was glad to come up and do the finishing work on the tower. He went up on a lift and put together a beautiful teakwood grill that covered the speakers on the four sides of the tower, and refused to take a penny

91

for his work. In no time, the carillons were calling people to Mass, playing hymns suitable for the whole liturgical year, as well as ecumenical hymns to everyone's joy. Our little parish of down-to-earth, unsophisticated people had worked hard to accomplish dreams that could make their parish a happy, joy-filled community whose spirit spread far from the parish, and made a difference in people's lives, not just the lives of their own people, but the lives of many others in the broader community.

But, the parish had such a high profile, it became like a lightning rod. At about that time, the State Crime Commission had decided to investigate certain conditions in the local community, to which I was not privy. Unfortunately, some prominent politicians in the community spread the rumor that I was behind the investigation, which was totally untrue. What prompted the rumor was the fact that one day a Crime Commission car was seen outside the rectory, and the persons who noticed it, spread the word that I was talking with them, which was not true. I was asked if I had any information about certain issues they were targeting. About those things I knew nothing so I could tell them nothing. Their questions were specific and my answers were specific and precise. Why they came to the rectory to talk to me was obvious, they watch television. They knew full well that I had been involved in the local communities for years, and thought I might have information about conditions in Amsterdam, and one of them involved certain criminal elements from New York City, whose tentacles reached as far as Amsterdam. About crime and criminals, I knew nothing. My interest was only in whatever would affect my parishioners, though some politicians and others were determined to blame me for the Crime Commission's presence. My people were my strongest defense, especially some of those who did gamble and knew everything that was going on in town and who was involved. They protected me against the troublemakers who were blaming me for the investigation. It was, still, a very difficult and frightening time. Word got back to me from some of my parishioners who had influential friends that the comment was being passed around, "Can't someone take care of that meddling priest? This place ran smooth till that guy came around."

Since then, life was no longer easy. For the first time, I made sure the doors and windows of the rectory were locked every night. The rectory was in a very vulnerable place at the edge of the city, and across the highway from the entrance to the thruway.

One night was particularly frightening. My lawyer and his wife had asked if I would baby sit for one of their kids, which was something they did every so often. Usually it was Joey, but this time it was Peter. Peter was about four at the time. They were super careful about baby sitters for their children, and when they couldn't get one of the few they trusted, they would ask me.

On the first night that Peter was with me, I heard someone working the lock at the back door. The noise was unmistakable. It was about one o'clock in the morning. I got out of bed, and quietly passed Peter's bedroom, and was walking down the creaky stairs when a voice called out, "Fahd, where are you going?"

"Peter get back into your room and don't make a sound. There's someone at the back door, and I don't want anything to happen to you."

"Fahd, I'll come down and protect you."

"Damn it, Peter, don't argue; get back into your room."

I could still hear someone picking at the lock, but when I got closer it stopped. I could see there was no one there. It is possible that since the back of the house was all glass, the light from the tall garden lamps shining through the windows and glass doors, cast my shadow around the rooms. Fortunately, nothing like that ever happened again, but it was a terrifying experience.

It was around this time that the construction of the synagogue was being completed. The whole community was happy for the Jewish people. The old synagogue had been standing for perhaps a hundred years, and it was very outdated. The new one was modest but modern and much larger than the previous one and built in very good taste. On the day of dedication, the whole Amsterdam community was well represented by clergy, politicians, important community leaders and friends of the Jewish people. It was a very happy occasion for all of us.

When I was asked to speak, it was a chance of a lifetime to say what I had been thinking over for many years. After expressing

94

the joy and excitement of my own parishioners at the Jewish people's great accomplishment in rebuilding their place of worship, I mentioned how close our two congregations had become over the past five years. Our friendships multiplied during that time, and we grew in understanding and caring for each other. Our two families had grown so close. It made me think of the earliest Christians who were all Jews, and the thought crossed my mind and I expressed it, that I could not see anything contradictory in my becoming a member of the Jewish community, and still remain pastor of Mount Carmel. Nor could I find it contradictory if any Jewish people believed in their hearts that Jesus was the Messiah, and became members of my parish, and still would be allowed to remain members of the synagogue. At the end of the ceremony I was surprised to see how many approved. Two orthodox rabbis came up to me afterward and said they could not see any real obstacles to such an arrangement.

Our two peoples were so close; it would have been the happy fulfillment of a dream if we could have made that a reality. A short time later, I asked the bishop if he had any objections to my making such a move. By that time we had a new bishop, a gracious man who was open to healthy changes in the Church. He thought the idea was mind-boggling and he would have to think about it.

Not long later, I decided to put the idea down on paper in the form of an eighteen-page proposal which I sent to the apostolic delegate, the pope's representative in Washington, since I had not heard from the bishop. He looked very favorably on the proposal and sent it to the department involved on a day-to-day liaison with the national Jewish committee. I received a very positive letter a short time later saying that officials saw nothing objectionable in the proposal and said that we have to start somewhere, and this might be just the way to start. With that approval, I approached a rabbi, Michael Szenes, with whom I had been friends for years, since our time on the Human Rights Commission together, and I asked him if I could become a member of his synagogue. (Rabbi Bloom's wife had died by this time, and Rabbi Bloom himself was not well, so I did not want to discuss the subject with him.)

Rabbi Szenes' reaction surprised me. "Why do you ask me?"

"Because I know you understand, and you are more liberal."

"But, Father Joseph, I am not really liberal. I may be the rabbi of a reform synagogue, but I go to an orthodox synagogue for my own personal services. I would have no problem if you came to my services all the time, but I do not feel comfortable making you a member of the congregation, especially as I am about to retire and it would put my successor in a difficult position."

After that I had no hope that I could do it, but at least the way was paved for anyone in the future to feel free to pursue that course, as a way of bringing two communities into a beautiful relationship. But, I also had a deeper reason for wanting to accomplish this. Having been in various communities over the years, I had always come in contact with Jewish people. During my first five years as a priest, I was assigned to a parish in the Bronx, where there were eight Jews to every Catholic in the neighborhood. We had excellent relationships with the Jewish people. In that parish, there were well over a 100 parishioners who were Jewish. One family were Hungarian Jews whom the United States government brought here, as the husband was a nuclear physicist, and the government needed atomic scientists for research. At the same time, I was asked if I would be on the board of the Edith Stein Guild, founded to honor that famous German Jewish phenomenologist philosopher, who had become a Catholic, and eventually a Carmelite nun, and eventually died as a martyr at Auschwitz. With that group, a whole new world of Jewish Catholics opened to me, as well as members of Edith Stein's family. My relationship with Jewish people was warm and very friendly.

One of the most touching relationships with Jewish people was with Harry and Jenny Zischoltz, who had a newsstand at the corner of the Grand Concourse and 182nd Street, in The Bronx. They were a beautiful old couple, still working right to the end, serving the neighborhood with their newspapers. One day I got a phone call from Jenny. "Father, can you please come up to the apartment right away. Harry is dying and he wants to see you." I immediately ran up the street in my monk's robes and into the apartment house which was all Jewish, and up to Harry and Jenny's place. Harry was lying on the couch, looking very weak and so frail.

"Harry, I am sorry; I didn't realize you were so sick. I would have come up sooner."

"Father, it happened suddenly, and when I knew I was dying, I wanted so much to see you and pray with you before I die. I got down on my knees next to his couch, and Jenny did the same and we prayed together. When we finished, we hugged each other, and Harry said in a very weak voice, "Good bye, Father, and my dear Jenny," and he died a short time later. I will never forget that touching moment, and every time I think of it, I cry.

At the end of my stay in The Bronx, I was sent to the coal mining region of Pennsylvania, in Pottsville, where I taught in a high school, and took chemistry courses at Albright, a Lutheran college, in Reading in the evening. On Friday nights, I took the students in my religion class to the Orthodox synagogue for their services, so they could understand what Jesus experienced as a young boy attending religious services in his day. The ceremony has not changed in all those intervening years. By the end of the school year, they had a good idea of what Jesus learned as a young Jewish boy, and what Jewish life was like even in his day.

Having seen how open Jewish people were to learning about Jesus, when I spoke in the synagogue, I could see they made a clear distinction between learning about Jesus, and the Christian churches, and I could see that there was an interest in learning more about him if we could share with them what their Jewish Jesus was like, and did not try to proselytize.

It then dawned on me, way back then, that if Jewish people wanted to follow Jesus as their messiah by becoming his disciples, could not the Church expand its vision to allow Jewish people and their rabbi to be accepted in the Church, keep their synagogue, and have properly ordained priests, of Jewish descent, be their pastor? In this way they could have their own ritual, and way of offering Mass, as we allow other cultures, and the Jewish people could then be assured of their Jewish identity forever in the future. Otherwise, the way society is working, more and more Jewish people are being absorbed and assimilated into the communities around them, by marriage or just by cultural interchange which draws them farther and farther from their own people until one day their numbers will dwindle to insignificance. I hope this plan is considered seriously by those of both religions who have mutual caring for each other's communities.

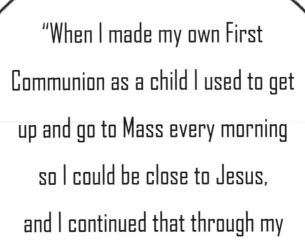

"When I made my own First
Communion as a child I used to get
up and go to Mass every morning
so I could be close to Jesus,
and I continued that through my
whole life."

Chapter Eight

With all that was happening in the community, we were still excited about happenings in the parish. Over time, attendance was growing. What was always important for me was to attract young people. Parents were so happy that their children home from college were coming to Mass and enjoying the experience. What was particularly encouraging was the number of young fellows with beards and long hair who started attending on a regular basis. Girls were always more responsible, but seeing the boys was heartening. Some were parishioners, some were strangers. Also, and what was particularly heartwarming for me was the how seriously little children were taking their religion. Often little ones not older than seven or eight would walk up to church even if their parents did not go to Mass. There was one little fellow whom I love dearly even after 30 years, because he touched my heart by the schemes he came up with to come to Mass. His family were always faithful parishioners, but little Jimmy who had Down's syndrome, would put on his swim trunks and go out in the backyard. Once in the yard he would leave there and walk up the street to the church. Then he would appear at the back of the church and when he spotted me up at the altar he would run up the aisle to the altar and, after giving me a hug, would ask if he could be my altar boy and serve my Mass. When I told him he could, but had to put on an altar boy's robe first, he would go in the sacristy, put on the robe and then come out to the altar. One time he put the robe on backwards with the hood in the front. I had to help him take it off and turn it around, and put it on again. He was so proud that he could serve Mass. And the nice thing about the incident, it was not a distraction for the people. Everyone knew the boy and they were all deeply impressed with that childlike faith. At the end Jimmy always asked, "Father, did I do a good job?" "Jimmy, it was the best," I told him.

Many years later, I spotted Jimmy and his mother at a talk I gave in Albany. When his mother told him I was going to be speaking, he asked if he could go with her. I was so happy I had a chance to spend some time with them afterwards.

There were other children in the parish who made me so happy when they came up to church alone, not that they were alone, but that they had the childlike faith and courage to come to Mass by themselves although their parents did not always go to church. One little girl, by the name of Stacy, wanted so much to make her First Communion, she walked up to Mass on Sunday morning faithfully. It was so beautiful. The last I heard of her is that she lives in Las Vegas, and is working there. I hope she is as faithful to Communion now as she was as a child.

I think perhaps the reason why the children enjoyed Mass so much was that they were asked to come up and stand around the altar with me at the offertory time. They loved that and, though they would tug on my robe and ask questions occasionally, the parish thought it was so good for the children. There were usually about

30 of them, and I am sure that Jesus used to let the kids come right up near him, and it was all part of what he was trying to teach not just the children but the grownups too, the simple beauty of little children's faith. Their presence alone reflected messages he was trying to teach. Forty years later, those now grown up kids still remind me of those days. The fun I got out of it was when I would meet the fathers during the week, they would say, "What are you doing with the kids?"

"Why?" I asked.

"Because they wake me up every Sunday when I'm trying to sleep and pester the heck out of me to take them to church. And they don't stop until I get out of bed."

"Good, aren't you proud of your child?"

"No, I'm as mad as ..."

"Good," and I'd laugh, "so scripture is right when it says, 'and a little child will lead them.'" It was all in good fun. It also served to get the men to take their responsibilities seriously, at least as far as the kids were concerned, even though the kids had to be their conscience. And in time a lot of the fathers started coming to Mass with the family.

But, getting some people to go to Mass was a difficult problem, as it is in most parishes. Eventually, by being persistent in letting them know you care, they start drifting back. Each week a few more would come. Some pastors complain about that at Mass, but those they are talking about aren't at Mass, so complaining merely annoys the faithful ones who do come. What I decided to do right from the start was to write a letter in the weekly bulletin to all the parishioners, and each week write about some aspect of our faith, beginning with the existence of God, and over a three-year period, cover all our beliefs in a way that would make sense to people. The bulletin was sent out to all our parishioners who did not come to church to let them know we cared.

When I visited various parishioners, especially those who were not coming to Mass, I saw piles of bulletins near their telephones. "What are they?" I asked.

"Don't you recognize them, Father; they're your bulletins. I read them over and over. Even though I don't go to Mass very often, I can still say I am learning a lot about my faith." I had encountered that so many times in visiting parishioners; it made me feel that all that work each week was worthwhile, and that someday I might have the joy of seeing them come back to Mass.

Life in the parish was so enjoyable, I never felt a need to take a day off. Working in my garden was enjoyable, though it consisted only of tomatoes, squash, and sugar beets one summer. I was surprised how big the sugar beets grew, and that they were full of real sugar. The greens were like Swiss chard, and very good to eat. That was my recreation. I always felt that recreation was doing work one enjoyed doing.

Even though I was close to the parishioners and was always there when they needed me, I made it a point not to have favorites in the parish whom I would visit.

I would often visit the Della Rattas in Schenectady, or the Riggis in Scotia, who had become very dear friends over the years. John Della Ratta had been my first contact with his family. When John was only about three years old, he used to visit his grandparents who lived only two doors from the rectory of one of the parishes where I had been stationed. John used to ride his little tricycle up to the rectory and ask the cook if I was home. The cook would always call me, and when I came down to the entrance, this little fellow would ask me, "Fahd, would you like to take a ride with me on my tricycle?"

"I'd love to, John."

So he would take me for a ride down the street, which was quite an adventure. He was so pleased when he dropped me off back at the rectory. I enjoyed it too. Not long after that, Joe and Pete, John's two smaller brothers, became friends and as time went on, I would babysit, as Richard, the father, often had to go to court at night, and Elizabeth was organist for the parish I had just left. The deal was she would continue being the organist at that parish, if I would babysit for the kids, which I really enjoyed doing. After supper, John, Joe and Pete would sit with me on the sofa facing the fire in the fireplace, as I told them stories. Every week I would make up another story. Their favorite I think was about a little

Chinese boy by the name of Jo-Jon-Fun-Lo, who was bored living by himself as his parents worked day and night in their Chinese restaurant on the waterfront. One night as he was hanging around the restaurant where the sailors ate, they invited him to tour their ship. When he got on, the ship set sail, and Jo-Jon-Fun-Lo found himself about to set sail for a far-off land. That story got rather involved and I had to keep telling them what happened before I could get them to go to bed. Every week I told them a different story, now I wish I had recorded them, though maybe someday one of the boys may put them all on paper.

When Joe and Pete took turns coming up to the rectory in Amsterdam, for awhile I told them stories, but they soon outgrew storytelling. They then wanted to have a little party before they went to bed, and we had to invent something different each time. John missed out in those days; he was too big by then. Besides that, he had a lot of friends, and had a paper route. But, John didn't escape what I had been teaching him and his little brothers. I didn't have as much influence over the two older brothers Michael and Ricky. They were quite grown up; seventh and eighth graders, when I first met the family.

But, the nice thing about these two little ones, and John, too, was that they loved their religion. Their religion was not church; it was Jesus. Though they respected the church, it was Jesus who was their religion, and they never lost that focus. I will never forget an incident when John was a paper boy. An old retired General Electric engineer stopped John one day when he was delivering his paper, and out of a clear blue sky, said to John, "How are you, Johnny?"

"Good, Mr. Jones. How are you? I see you're getting some exercise today?"

"I'm just taking a little walk. It's no fun getting old. Life can be boring and lonely. You always seem to be so happy."

"I am happy. Life is fun."

"Do you believe in God?"

"Of course I do. That's why I'm happy.

"I can't believe there's a God."

"Maybe that's why you're lonely; you're all alone. I'd feel lonely, too, if I didn't believe in God. Friends don't help. Most friends are not real friends. They hurt a lot, especially when they make fun of you. Then I think God's my friend and I don't hurt."

"Thank you, young man. I'll have to think about that."

And some place it says in scripture, "And a little child shall lead them."

Even though John did not have the same closeness with me as he grew and had more and more outside activities, John was always caring, and thoughtful of others. He always did a lot of thinking and never let on how serious that little brain of his was, but it would reveal itself occasionally, like the time he asked his parents, "Did Fahd have to go to school to be a priest or did he just get hooked on religion?" I happened to be at the house the time and overheard him. I laughed and told him, "John, if you only knew how much school we had! We went to college even in the summertime, and even after I was ordained. I was 32 years old when I finally stopped going to school."

Later, John blossomed in law school by staying on the dean's list and then, after graduation, on passing his bar exam, he so impressed the examiners that they asked his permission to use his answers as model answers for the bar exam. He now has a reputation for taking on and winning very difficult cases which other lawyers turn down because they seemed impossible to win.

Teaching the Della Ratta boys their religion was good practice for me, and helped me understand what was important for the children in the parish to know about their religion. The children were always a most critical part of parish life and I tried so hard to come up with ways to present their faith to them that would remain with them forever. Holy Communion was most important in my mind, and I felt that what they are taught about Communion is an essential part of their faith, and has to be a natural expression of their parents' faith. Having strangers teach them about Communion always reminded me of a skin graft from a stranger that will never take. Faith has to be a natural part of family life, and should flow from the way the family lives and believes, not the way a stranger believes, and especially if it concerns Holy Communion.

So, what I did in the parish was hold classes for the parents, and teach them the most important aspects of their faith and how they should teach the children about Communion especially. Then after I had taught the parents, they had to prepare the children for their First Holy Communion. Some of the parents resented this intrusion on their lives, but I would not give in, and eventually they appreciated it, especially when they began to actually enjoy what I was teaching them.

As a family finished preparing their child, they would bring the child in to see me so I could question him or her about what they understood about Communion, and then I would casually introduce them to confession, which they had also been prepared for at home. It was done in a very casual way, so they could enjoy telling me the childlike ways they did things that were not nice. They enjoyed telling me what they had done that was not nice, because it made them feel good inside and that they felt that God was now happy with them. Then I would give them absolution, and tell them that they had just made their first confession. "That was fun, Father," some would tell me. That made me happy when they said that, and I know they were good confessions because the matter was real. I could see them struggling with some things that were difficult for them. To see them peaceful afterwards was gratifying.

The following Sunday was special for that family. The whole family would come to whatever Mass they chose and sit up in the front row, and the mother and father would come up to receive

Communion with their son or daughter, and then the rest of their family. They all were expected to receive.

"But, I'm not Catholic, Father."

"Do you believe what you taught your child?"

"Yes,"

"And you're at peace with God?"

"Yes, I think so."

"And you've been baptized?"

"Yes,"

"Well, what's your problem? It is critical that your child sees that you have a love for the Eucharist so it will always be beautiful for them and a natural part of their family's life."

"Father, you're tough."

"No, I'm too easy, and I get into trouble for it. You will be proud someday, knowing that your children are following your good example."

Confirmation was also a sacrament that I had often felt was not properly approached when the young people were being prepared. It was a sacrament they received at high school age. So, even though it took time in my schedule that was already tight, this was important to me, so I taught the Confirmation class myself. The thrust of the preparation process was intimacy with Jesus, and getting to know the real Jesus, and getting the students to understand themselves and where they were in their faith journey.

A good part of each class was helping the students to know Jesus, who he was, what he was about, how he is a most important part of their young lives, and is in fact their best friend. After a year of attempting to deepen the students' understanding of who Jesus is, and what he should mean to them, I explained that Confirmation was not just another stepping stone in their social life, where the family has another party, but Confirmation was making a lifetime commitment to Jesus as their best friend, and the one person whom they wanted to be their partner for the rest of their life. In doing this, they were also asking for the Holy Spirit to continue His work of deepening Jesus' life in their soul. I also stressed that this commitment should not be taken lightly, and if they do not feel they would like to make that commitment to Jesus that is their right, and that they should not feel any pressure to do so. Also, if anyone did not feel ready to make that commitment yet, that person should not be embarrassed to say so. And I promised to back them up if their parents were upset about their choice.

When the time for the bishop to come for Confirmation, only one person told me she felt she was not ready yet, and was struggling trying to feel if she was ready to make such a commitment. I felt very bad, because if there was anyone in that class that I felt was ready, it was that girl. But, her sincerity had a profound effect on the other students, because they all knew her, and her seriousness in approaching the sacrament, deepened the sincerity of the others' commitment.

When the Confirmation took place and the bishop came and spoke to the students, I was proud of the intelligent answers they gave to questions the bishop asked. The ceremony went well and I could tell the parents were proud of their sons and daughters and how seriously they took their commitment to Jesus. A month later, the girl who postponed hers, called and said she felt she was finally ready. I was so happy, and so was she. I made arrangements for her to make her Confirmation at a special ceremony for adults at the Cathedral in Albany. She was thrilled, and the next day she wore her Confirmation dress to the public high school she attended, which made her stand out, because like the others, she always wore casuals. The principal who was a lector at our parish asked her if she wasn't embarrassed that she might stand out. The principal told me later how she responded, "But, isn't that what Confirmation is all about, being proud of what you are, and not being ashamed to profess it, even in a symbolic way." He told me how impressed he was.

If this recounting of the things that took place in the parish seems disjointed, it is a perfect mirror of what parish life was like when a pastor is open to the people. At about this time, a doctor whom I had known called to tell me a patient had given birth and would be totally unable to care for the baby. The doctor asked if I knew a worthy couple who were unable to have children and would be willing to adopt this baby. I knew a perfect couple. I made arrangements for the doctor to meet with the couple and the adoption went very smoothly. That baby now is in his thirties, a beautiful young man and a teacher in one of the area schools.

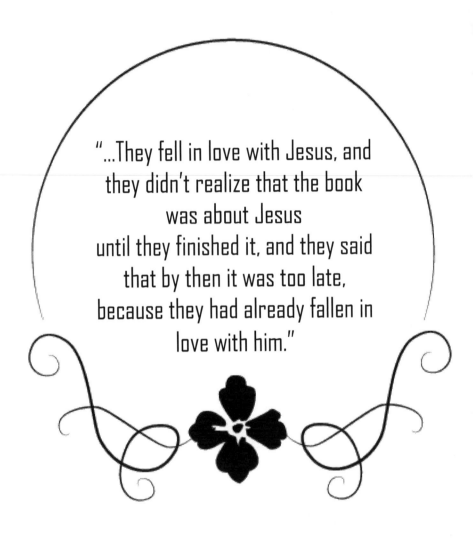

"...They fell in love with Jesus, and
they didn't realize that the book
was about Jesus
until they finished it, and they said
that by then it was too late,
because they had already fallen in
love with him."

Chapter Nine

The city of Amsterdam is a very old city, founded as part of a town called Caughnawaga around 1788. It was later called Veedersburg, and was incorporated as a city in 1885, when presumably its first charter was approved. For many years, it was considered the carpet capital of the country, and had a population at that time of close to 35,000 people. The Erie Canal passed along the downtown area of the city. The population of Amsterdam was originally Dutch, but later Irish, Italians, Germans, Poles, and Lithuanians made Amsterdam pretty much a reflection of the population of America itself. Lately a large community of Hispanics has become a sizeable part of the population of Amsterdam.

Because of the changing demographics, especially the significant drop in the population of the city, due to the exodus of the carpet mills, the 1885 charter had become totally obsolete, and cried out for a change. The city finally formed a Charter Revision Commission to review the 1885 Charter and revise it. I think there were originally seven members of the Commission, with John Betz, a popular funeral director in town, as the Chairman, and I as the Co-Chairman.

At our first meeting, we had already obtained copies of the 1885 Charter, and when reading it carefully, it did not take long to discourage us. When, for example, the Charter talked about controlling traffic on the main street of the city, it was not talking about cars and trucks, but the flow of chickens, sheep and other animals. In the charter, the city had been laid out in nine wards. That was when the population was almost double its present size. In time that made it possible for a person to be elected as an alderman with only a few more votes than the number of relatives he or she had. Talking to John Betz, after our first meeting, he asked what I thought we should do. I felt that it would be impossible to make little changes here and there. I told him, "It is like taking pieces out of a quilt and trying to find patches that will match. Since we are a Commission and not a Committee, we can do what we want with it." John said he didn't know anything about charters, and I certainly knew nothing about charters, but, I suggested we write a whole new charter, and make our effort worthwhile. It was one chance in 100 years to make a significant change in the political life of the city, and we can relieve the financial burden on the city and cut out a lot of the closed-door deals. We both thought it was ridiculous that the Public Works Director was a truck driver, and the licensed city engineer was just one of his employees. This made it possible for the politicians to hire their friends as contractors when city work had to be done, and at taxpayers' expense. Why not make the city engineer the Commissioner of Public Works and let him train his crew to do city work without having to hire outsiders. It would be a huge savings to the taxpayers.

We finally managed to convince the other members that we should write a completely new charter. At first they panicked. "We don't know anything about writing charters." I suggested we start by calling heads of the various city departments and asking them what changes they would like to see in their departments. They agreed and we called in the mayor and the members of the city council, and the corporation counsels, and asked for their input. After getting a massive amount of information from practically everyone we could think of, we then had to make a decision as to what we would do next. John Betz and I became best of friends during this whole time, as we had to sweat out each new move we made. The legal aspects of a charter we knew nothing about, so we decided to contact the New York State Charter Revision office, and ask if they could help us. "Sure can, that's what we're here for." What a relief! They offered all kinds of help mostly with suggestions, but left all the details of what we wanted for our city up to ourselves. They told us not to be discouraged, even though most new charters are voted down by the people when they are submitted at election time. That was something else we had to consider. But, at least we had ready access to the state experts all the remaining time while we worked on the details of the charter.

We reduced the number of wards to five from the original nine, because of the radical drop in population. This would certainly upset the politicians, not only in the city but in the county, where adjustments would have to be made there as well. In the old charter, the city water department was just part of the city government, and since it took in considerable sums of money each year, it had more than enough money to continually update and

117

repair the water works throughout the city. Unfortunately, it had become the slush fund for the city officials. Money to repair water pipes came from the homeowners who had to pay to have not just the area from their house to the sidewalk dug up, but the street as well, which was most unfair. So, in the charter we made the water department a separate entity which should have control over its own money, and use that money to repair broken pipes and bring the water supply up to proper health department requirements, to assure the highest quality of drinking water.

Other matters in the new charter tightened up the way ordinary city business was done to prevent sloppy management, and purchasing practices. In the old ways, practically any employee in any city department could buy something and send the bill to the department. This totally frustrated any attempt at maintaining and observing a budget. Also, when it came to bids for jobs, we felt it was much better for bids not to be kept in the safe at city hall, but that all bids should be kept in a bank, and delivered to city hall the day they were to be opened in public. There were many other minor details, but the whole charter was put together in a little over a year. When we finished, we asked the state experts to look it over thoroughly for us to make sure everything was legal, made sense, was do-able, and practical. After several their people scrutinized every word of it, they called and told us they could not believe this was done by amateurs. They highly commended each member of our Commission, and said they could recommend it if we needed their support.

We still had a few months left before the November election. The next step was to submit our work to the newspaper for the new charter to be printed as a supplement to the daily edition of the paper. A few days later the charter was in the hands of every person in the city, including all the city officials. Since it was quite a good size document, it was not a thin supplement that was inserted in the newspaper. The reaction was immediate. The people who took time to read it thought it was very well done, especially those parts where they knew they would be saving money. The politicians were furious, and immediately filled the Amsterdam Recorder, the local newspaper, with criticisms and objections to it. They did everything they could to scuttle it.

Finally, I talked with John Betz about all the opposition, and suggested that we challenge them to a public debate. John laughed and said, "You are most welcome to it, but I'm afraid you'll have to do it on your own. I am not into those kinds of things." So, I challenged the city officials to a televised debate which the whole city could watch. The TV channel gave us two hours. When the time came, I was there alone. None of the city officials showed up. So, I had a great time; two hours with the old charter on one knee and the new charter on the other knee. And I compared each provision and explained the reason for each change.

One other critical move that had to be done was to get significant support. Congressman Sam Stratton, who lived in Amsterdam, was highly respected by people in both parties. Sam was a democrat, and a very conservative chairman of the armed services committee of Congress. Sam and I were good friends, and whenever I needed his help for difficult situations he was always ready to help. At one time a person working at the GE defense laboratory had a son who had gone to Canada to avoid the draft. The parents were beside themselves. When I called and asked if he would be willing to intercede for the young men involved, if I could talk them into coming back into the country, he was most gracious. The whole affair was worked out with dignity and compassion, but without compromising justice and principle.

Sam had been a mayor in the area previously, so he was most familiar with city charters. We sent him a copy of ours and a few days later I called him and asked what he thought of it, and if he felt it was practical and realistic. He was most enthusiastic and said it was sorely needed. I then asked him if he could endorse it. He said he would be glad to. So, I suggested he contact the local newspaper the morning of the day before the election, so the paper could include it in their evening edition. It turned out magnificently. The headline read. "Stratton Endorses New Charter" in bold print across the page. And if I am not mistaken, Brad Broyles was the one responsible for that big splash. It did the trick. The people had such a respect for Sam; his endorsement was all they needed. The next day at the close of the polls, the charter was approved by close to 79 percent of the voters. The following day we got a very happy phone call from the state people who helped us so much. They were beside themselves, because it was a feather in their cap, since so many of the local charters they worked on in other places were voted down by large majorities. It was a happy end to a very worthwhile undertaking that benefited the whole city. Our little group of amateurs felt so proud at being successful at something we originally knew nothing about. It was not an easy task. It was very hard work and any pride we had when we finished came from our realization that, in spite of our original total ignorance of the subject, we were able to finally produce a document that we knew would benefit the whole community for the next 100 years. I think it was more a feeling of relief when we finished than a feeling of pride that we had accomplished something great. John Betz, who had given so much of himself could go back to his position as funeral director, as could all the other dedicated commission members, who had sacrificed time, energy and brain power to provide important input into the final document.

When election returns came in and I realized the charter had passed by such a huge margin, I was happy, but when I went to bed, I cried, "Is this what a priest should be doing? Where have I failed? Why can't my life be normal, like other priests? And my memory went back to a day so many years before, when my mystical theology professor called me down to his room and asked me to explain a paper I had written, telling me he could not understand it. When I explained it to him, he said, "That is beautiful. What a fascinating way of understanding the mystical relationship between Jesus' mother and each one of us, especially those who belong to her Order of Carmel dedicated to her." He proceeded to tell me I had a rare speculative mind and that the Church needed speculative theologians, and asked if I would like to go to Rome for further studies in theology and mysticism, and teach there." I told him I would love that. Later on, he became the superior general of the Carmelites, and all I had to do was remind him. But, instead I said to myself, "No, I will never politick. I will let the Holy Spirit do with me whatever he wills."

And now, realizing that I was so far removed from what had been my dream as a young theologian, I felt I had failed somehow, and it made me review my whole priesthood. From that day, I vowed never to politick; my life was never the same. It has been a most horrible succession of painful, though also many happy, experiences, which placed me in situations and circumstances for which I had no experience, situations that tested my faith, my vocation as a priest, my sanity, and even my ability to survive. I did not feel I was doing the work of a priest most of the time. Circumstances far beyond my control forced me into situations that I had to respond to, but situations which were not part of a normal priest's job description, and all of which made me feel like a misfit, an oddball, and I knew that is what so many thought of me. I felt totally that I just did not fit, and I began to go deep into myself and try to understand where I had gone wrong, and what was wrong with me, and why I could not be like everyone else. I was afraid to make friends because I felt they had to see that I was odd. I missed the monastic life. All I had wanted was to spend my life studying and I would have loved to write and teach theology and prepare young men for their priesthood. That life would have been so peaceful and tranquil and would have had meaning for me. But, all I did as a priest was run into one crisis after another, not necessarily church related crises, but crises in the cities and government institutions, crises in situations for which I had no training or expertise, which made me frequently wonder if my life as a priest was a failure.

I tried to pray, but it was always hard for me to pray outside of the monastery. The monastery chapel and the monastery grounds were like a piece of heaven on earth. It was like holy ground. God's presence was real. Praying as you walked along a busy street, or during involvement with politicians, or sitting waiting in a warden's office was no comparison to a monastic chapel. In my parish, I would walk around the church grounds as night through the flowering trees and talk to God in a very simple but unsatisfying way. So often I felt that God was far away, and I was in exile, and all I could do was cry. Maybe my tears were my prayers. The only comfort I had was from a feeling way deep down inside me that my every move had a purpose, but the feeling was so deep down that it was hard to understand its meaning. How could all these endless disconnected events have meaning when they seemed like chance happenings in a life that was utterly disconnected?

How could the orderly God work in such a disorderly life, and in a way that seemed to make no sense at all? How can God even know what is going on in anyone's life with all the billions of people there are in the world? And who am I to be so special that God should know every detail of my life, or that he should even care? They were my thoughts one night when I went over to the church at midnight to make sure everything was locked. On the way back to the rectory, as I was walking along the path through the flowering plum trees, a beautiful thought struck me: God's mind is like the sunrise in the morning. As the rays of the morning sun shoot across the universe, they touch all of creation in a single instant. When God's mind scans his creation, it is like the rays of the sun, touching all of creation in a single moment and immediately knowing every detail about every creature throughout the whole universe. It was all so simple. I felt as if God had been listening to my thoughts all along and finally gave me an important insight into his own omniscience. Maybe there was after all a purpose. When I reached the rectory, I tried to write down what I had experienced but I could not find words, nothing was anywhere near adequate to describe that flash of insight that so profoundly affected me. All I could do was thank God for letting me know he knew and he cared.

Chapter Ten

Winter was upon us and one day the snow kept falling endlessly since the night before. Almost 18 inches of snow made it impossible for many workers to leave the city for out of town work. I am sure Gilda came, and Tony, who cleared the sidewalks and the parking lot which by that time was rented by the state for their employees who worked in Albany. Our little Office on Aging staff showed up. God bless them. They were so dedicated.

There was nothing for me to do, so I lighted a fire in the fire place and put on the classical music station, WMHT, and said what a wonderful day to write a book. I didn't have a computer then. They were not out yet. So, I got a legal-size writing pad and pen and started to write. It was my first manuscript, "Kara, The Lonely Falcon." It was an allegory on our search for peace, inner peace, peace with others, peace among nations and most importantly, peace with God. I used the falcon as the symbol of human nature. Falcons are sleek, fast and deadly, as so many humans can be when we use others to get ahead or for personal reasons. For peace, it is necessary to find peace within ourselves first, then we are well positioned to be at peace with others, and to help others find peace. As I was writing I noticed that as the story progressed, I was writing at two, then three different levels, and that the reader would naturally become aware of the different levels, and would have to be able to follow through on each of those different levels. Then I had to follow the story myself at each of those levels to make sure that each story would have its own direction and own conclusion. By the end of the day I had finished the manuscript. It was only about sixty pages long. I had finally done something that I felt was in some way priestly, and might help people to find peace. I couldn't get it published so I paid a vanity press to publish it, but found out they don't promote the books they publish, so I had to sell it myself, and had a hard time because the industry boycotts the products of those publishers. In time though, it sold when published by Macmillan and was eventually translated into Chinese, Japanese, Croatian and other languages.

Around this time, a religious sister, Sister Lucy Tubbs, who was working with the Spanish speaking community in Amsterdam, called and asked if she could meet with me. She was a woman in the sixties and a Sister of Saint Joseph. I had known her for years after she had returned from South America where she worked for close to 25 years. She was totally dedicated to the Spanish speaking people and had been hired by Catholic Charities in Amsterdam to work with the Latino community, translating for them in court proceedings, and in dealing with local government offices. I knew of her work and how dedicated she was to it. When she came to the rectory, she was in tears, telling me that she had been fired by the agency, and that a very negative report was put in her file. She was totally devastated, and wanted to know if she could please work with me, perhaps teaching the children and working with the elderly. She didn't even want a salary, just to be able to continue doing worthwhile work with people who needed her. I told her we could really use her talents. But I also thought that she should not just accept being fired. She should appeal to the new Due Process Board that had been set up by the diocese. I asked her if her community would back her up and she assured me they would. So, while working in the parish by visiting the sick elderly, bringing them Communion and spending time with them, and teaching the children religion, she proved to be of valuable help to the community. In the meantime, after a year of delay and me expressing strongly my unhappiness about the incompetent way her case was handled, she finally won her case and the agency that fired her was ordered to offer her job back, which she did not want. The agency was also ordered to pay her back salary which the diocesan officials said they could not afford, so she settled just to have her unfair reports expunged from her file. The adjudicator who, finally, was a professional, ordered that the diocese should pay her something. Right after that, she went to live at her motherhouse and a year or two later she died, a real dedicated saintly soul.

It was also at that time that one of her sisters at Saint Mary's Hospital called, and said there were seventy-some South Vietnamese refugees who were on their way to Amsterdam. The sister said she had asked all the other parishes if they would sponsor their coming.

Unfortunately, there was no way they could see their way clear to committing themselves to such a responsibility. The sister said we were their last hope, and could we please help. I told her our parish was unable to even consider any new expenses. We were in horrible shape financially. All the programs in the parish were run only on support from outside sources. She said it would not entail any outlay of funds, just to care for their spiritual welfare, provide them with a place to go to Mass and feel welcomed by the parishioners, and also prepare the children for baptism and First Communion. I said that would be no problem. Our people were so warm and friendly; they would be more than happy to welcome them and befriend them. A few days later they arrived, and a priest from one of the other parishes went to meet them at the airport, which I found out later and which I could not understand because he was one of the pastors who said he could not sponsor them at his parish. A few hours later they were all settled in at the two or three grand mansions the Sisters at the hospital had all ready for them. From that day and for the next couple of years they were welcomed as members of Our Lady of Mount Carmel parish. Our people were not only inspired by their deep piety, but were especially impressed by the very reverent way they approached the Eucharist. Our people fell in love with them and made them feel very much a part of everything we did in the parish. We all benefited greatly from the warm relationship we had with them. It was interesting as we got to know them more intimately. They were mostly fish eaters, and one day when I was driving down the highway I saw a whole group of them spreading fishnets across the shallow part of the Mohawk River, to catch their food for supper. They like to catch their own fish, to make sure it is fresh. One day I took a few of them to a fish market, and as soon as we walked in, they asked to leave. I asked them why, and they said, "We can smell the fish, and good fish you cannot smell, that is why we were fishing in the river." I don't think they were allowed to do it anymore, but our people were generous in helping them in whatever way we could especially at Christmas and Easter.

As much as we came to love those wonderful families, they could not bear our bitterly cold winters up our way, and a year and a half later they went to Louisiana, where the weather was more to what they were used to, and where they would be in fishermen's paradise.

With our parish welcoming all these Vietnamese families and treating them with such love was a blessing not only for the parish but for me as well. At last, it made me feel that I was being a part of some good priestly work, and that together with the Office on Aging, made it possible for us to reach out to so many hundreds of hurting people not just in our parish but in the wider community. And it was not just our own people, but people from other congregations, Catholic, Protestant and Jewish, who worked on the programs for the elderly throughout the county. They could all feel they were following God's command to care for the hungry, the thirsty, the sick, the lonely, those imprisoned in their homes, often all alone. They were all being God's heart and hands and lips to those who needed nourishment for their bodies, and comfort for their souls. Though they did all the work, I felt that in some small way I was contributing something that could be considered priestly work, if only by signing documents and encouraging those who were spending so much of themselves doing all the work. I was surprised the number of people who came to the meal sites, not just for food, but to meet friends, and have some companionship, and the great numbers who were living alone and were waiting eagerly for their day's meal and evening snack, when otherwise they might have gone hungry and eventually died from malnutrition. For the first time, I realized what a wonderful ministry for a parish to run such a program, where they could reach out to all the hurting elderly in the whole wide territory, and care for so many people, a different way of putting into real life practice the corporal and spiritual works of mercy, following Jesus' instruction to his disciples.

Was it all just good works for the sake of good works? No, not at all. These people were inspired by their deep faith and concern for others. Jesus worked day and night, curing, healing, giving life, and sight and wholeness to others. Were his works a waste? It was the way he expressed his love, by caring and healing, and inspiring those who needed him. Our work was the same. It was the expression of our faith which inspired the people to give of themselves to express their commitment to Jesus' command to love God and one another, as a proof of the sincerity of their faith.

The bishop about that time had issued a pastoral letter to the diocese. It was contained in an insert in the diocesan newspaper. The parishioners read it very carefully to see if I was doing things according to the bishop's stated ideals. It seems they were always measuring me against what they felt were the standards, which sprang from their cultural distrust of clergy. I was surprised that they would take the time to read the letter, especially since it was so long.

At the next parish council meeting, one of the members said to me, "The bishop must be really proud of you."

"Why?" I asked.

"Because we have already been doing everything he said parishes should do."

I said nothing. They had no idea the trouble I was in with the diocese, and how little the diocese valued anything that was being done in our parish. Why should I upset them even more than they were already by sharing with them my problems? I had spent six hard years trying to heal long-standing wounds caused by insensitive bishops. They were coming out of that which made me feel good that they had a much lighter attitude toward the Church.

There were a lot of light moments in the parish during those busy days. As little Joey Della Ratta, my godson, was growing up, he was becoming a very good pianist. As young as he was, about eight or nine at that time, he could play the piano with grace and ease. It was a joy to listen to him. His teacher, Mr. Hummel, was a famous concert pianist who expected great things from the boy. Even though Joey was so young, his talent as a musician was extraordinary, though Mr. Hummel was concerned because Joey started arriving at his house with his baseball uniform and glove. I suppose I was partially to blame for that. It was about that time that Joey used to come to Amsterdam more frequently so I could teach him how to play baseball, which I would do after supper. First I taught him how to catch fly balls, grounders, and line drives which I would throw in his direction. Then, he wanted to learn how to use a bat. This was sort of dangerous, not for him, but for me. I stood too close and in the beginning, pitched underhand, until he could get his eye on the ball. Then when he became consistent in hitting the ball practically every time I threw it, I stepped back and pitched over hand, which was a little faster. After 15 or 20 times, he began to connect, and one time, he hit a line drive right at me. I hardly had time to duck. Next time, I stepped back about 15 feet and threw the ball faster, and soon he was hitting long shots way out close to 50 yards. He finally had it all down, and the following week, he was accepted on a team. I had seen him play only once. When he hit the ball, it went way out to left center field. He had arrived, and he was good, and he could run like a little deer. But, Mr. Hummel was beginning to realize where Joey's heart was, and he was very disappointed when Joey switched from piano to trumpet, which he used to practice endlessly. Sometimes he would go up on the roof of his folk's house and sit on the peak of the roof and practice his trumpet, "the fiddler on the roof."

One day when he went to practice on the roof, he saw a police car parked in front of the house. The car was parked facing the end of the median separating both sides of the street. Joey didn't care for the police because some of them were mean to some of his friends. One of his friends who was an excellent pianist and often accompanied Joey in gigs, was not allowed to practice at home because it disturbed his father. So, he would go down to the Union College chapel and practice on the piano there. One night he was arrested for trespassing and I think he was taken to jail. Joey's father represented him, and eventually got the boy off, but that incident and other incidents bothered Joey.

So, when Joey saw the police car outside his house, he recognized the policeman as one who was not very nice. Joey put a few eggs in his pocket and went up on the roof to practice. The police car was about a hundred feet from where he was perched on the peak of the roof. When he stopped to give his lip a rest, he took out an egg and with his uncanny aim, threw the egg down at the police car and hit the windshield, then started playing the trumpet again. The policeman got out to clean the egg off the windshield, and by then Joey was innocently playing the trumpet, as if nothing had happened. This happened three times. The policeman at first thought it was a bird in the tree above, but later suspected it must have come from the roof across the street, but had no proof, because that kid seemed so interested in his music. Joey never confessed.

He was such a lovable kid, but sometimes I worried about him because he was innocent, and so vulnerable. I also felt he was a very lonely boy, and I could feel his pain. One Friday he came to Amsterdam, and stayed over the weekend. After Mass on Sunday, we were driving back to his folk's house for dinner. On the way he had picked up the remote for the garage door, and started calling a friend by the name of Mack. "JFD calling MAK come in Mack."

Then he would hold a conversation with Mack. I knew kids who used to do things like that, and for the most part they were lonely kids who had no friends, and invented imaginary friends. But I knew Joey had a lot of friends. Then the thought crossed my mind that perhaps Joey was just a lonely little fellow in spite of all his friends. I asked him if Mack talked back when he talked to him. "Of course, Fahd. He always talks to me. He's my best friend, after you." "Will he talk to me if I talk to him?" "Of course, Fahd," he said as he handed me the garage door opener. I talked to Mack, and waited and waited, and no answer. "Joe, Mack doesn't answer." "Oh, I forgot to tell you, Fahd, Mack's mother told him not to talk to strangers."

Still worried about his need for a make-believe friend, I took off my watch and asked if he would like to wear it. "Yeah, Fahd, I love that watch." It was a beautiful watch a group gave me years before as a present when I left their parish.

134

Later on, after dinner at the Della Ratta's, before I left to go back to Amsterdam, I asked Joe if I could have the watch back. He acted very strangely, and I could not figure out why. It was to take many years before I found out the reason.

For the rest of the time I was in Amsterdam, Joe and Pete used to love to come and visit. They were a lot of fun. Lena loved them, and I think she had a special love for Pete. "He is one classy young man," she used to say. "He's like a little German, knows just what he wants and don't try to stop him. You watch, he's a smart boy." Pete loved Lena, and especially her chicken soup, which is still his favorite meal, a big bowl of chicken soup.

Whenever I had to go to a wake when the kids were there, I had to find a babysitter. Either Gilda or Diane, Gilda's daughter, would come to the rectory and babysit for whichever one was visiting, or they would go to their house down the street, while I went to the wake. Gilda was a dear friend during those times, as well as my loyal assistant. Pete was not much of a problem, though he always pestered to go with me to the funeral parlor. I was reluctant to bring either him or Joey to see a corpse. I did not know how it would affect kids. Joey wouldn't say anything when I left, but he was terribly upset while I was gone. I never realized how attached those two kids were to me. When Joey was at Gilda's he apparently was not too nice, but Gilda understood, and it never bothered her. I don't know what I would have done in the parish without her. She was very bright and had so many complicated projects to monitor and track in order to keep her financial records in perfect order; I don't know how she did it. And she was always so gracious. I doubt if I could have even found anyone who would have been so understanding and so efficient, even in the most difficult times for the parish, with all we went through.

Another happy event in those days was the coming of a Chinese family to Amsterdam. The building inspector, Ed, the one who had come to me about the housing problems, stopped over for a visit. He and his family had become dear friends. They lived over in the Polish neighborhood across the river. On this visit, he had some good news to tell me. "Your Chinese friends are opening a restaurant over on the hill. They want to invite you to the open house." That Chinese family were very special. I had taught their two children English when they first come to the States from Hong Kong. I had tried to encourage them to open a restaurant in Amsterdam, but they were reluctant at first, concerned that there might not be enough customers. Well, they finally came and were opening up in a couple of weeks. I was delighted because I loved Chinese food and these people were excellent chefs. I and my friends were invited to the opening. The food they served was absolutely gourmet, Chinese style, and made a deep impression on all the local people who came. I told them that night that the restaurant was too small. Eventually, they bought and renovated another place out on the highway. It was a beautiful place, six times the size or the one they left, and it became so popular that the diners had to wait in the bar section for at least half an hour before they could be seated. I was so happy for these dear friends.

Later on, I was invited to the daughter's wedding, which was performed in the church in the next town, Hagaman. Moon Wing, the boy, had been in the army and had an interesting assignment, repairing high tech instruments and vehicles. When he came home, he would stop off at the parish on Sunday mornings to visit, and asked if I would teach him how to drive. I was like a father to that boy, as his father was always working in the restaurant. I taught him how to drive while another priest was offering Mass in church. After a few Sundays, Moon Wing was off on his own. The next time I saw him was when he called up one day and said he was getting married. When I asked him when, he said, "Right now, this afternoon." I could not believe it. I asked him who he was marrying, and he told me, "A girl from Hong Kong." I think the match may have been arranged. Since I couldn't do it, I called a local judge, Judge Catena, whose family were friends and asked if he could help. He also was shocked, but we went ahead with the ceremony at the judge's house. Afterward, we were invited to the little party, just Moon Wing, his mother, his bride, the judge and I. I think his sister may have been there also. I felt bad it was all so simple, I was learning how different people's customs can be.

One of the waitresses at the restaurant was a friend of the owner's family, and also a dear friend of mine. I don't think I have ever seen a more beautiful woman, tall and stately. Her husband was a geologist who lived in Taiwan and worked for the government, so she had free time on her day off, so she offered to teach a course in Chinese cooking, for people in my parish. Quite a good number of my friends took the course, which lasted for about six months. The course was part of the program we had at our empty school, where other subjects were taught as well, like Russian and Chinese, as I felt that this would be a great asset sometime in the future, and added more excitement to the parish. I felt bad when a few years later, after the Chinese boy and girl were married, the parents closed the restaurant, and moved. I have since lost contact with them, and miss their friendship. I had been very much a part of their life since they came to this country. Moon Wing's sister was a beautiful young lady and learned English faster than Moon Wing, who was a real comedian in my class. When I asked him if he was going to college, he said, "Of course."

"But, I thought you hated school?"

"I do, but I'm not stupid. I don't want to get stuck in a Chinese restaurant for the rest of my life."

About this time, things were beginning to change in Amsterdam. One day, two of my parishioners called and were upset with me because they had heard news about our parish which I had not shared with them. "What are you keeping from us, Father?" Pat Zumbolo burst out with his booming voice over the telephone.

"I don't know what you're talking about, Pat. You had better tell me, if you know something I don't."

"That big mouth across the river," Pat bellowed out, "was at the bowling alley last night, and was telling us he is going to be pastor of Mount Carmel."

"If he is, I haven't heard a thing about it, so it's just what you said it is, his 'big mouth.' You know I share everything with you all, except my own personal dealings with the diocese, and I handle that myself."

"I know that, and we admire you for that. But, are you telling me that what he said is not true?"

"Pat, I never heard about it, if it is true. I think it's just a crock of bull."

It turned out, however, that what Pat heard was pretty near the truth, though it was over a month later that I found out about it, when the bishop called me to the chancery office, and said he was going to merge Saint Michael's and Mount Carmel. Obviously, he had been talking to the pastor of Saint Michael's, the other Italian parish, and it also seemed that he had told the pastor that he would be the pastor of the two merged parishes, though the bishop never shared that with me. And now that he finally called me he merely told me that the two parishes would be merged. I was shocked but I knew it made sense, so I told him it was a wise move as the population of the city had shrunk by over thirty percent, and there was no reason why there should be seven parishes for less than 18,000 people. I also suggested that there could be three parishes considered in the merger, so he would not have to go through the trauma again in the future. I told him I would support him on this since it made sense and had to done, as painful as it would be for all of us.

The upshot of that meeting was that he later called the pastor of Saint Michael's, the pastor of Saint John's, the German parish, and me to the chancery and told us that he had made a decision to merge our parishes. He also told us that this would take place in July, which was four months away. He also told us that we were not to tell the people about it until July. I had no problem with that. I knew something like this would have to be done sooner or later. I did suggest, however, that when that date arrived, he should have each of us reassigned immediately. He asked why, and I told him that if he was going to tell the people that he was forced to do this because there was a shortage of priests, then when the merger took place, and we were just floating around with no assignments it was going to make him look ridiculous for not telling the truth about a shortage of priests. He agreed.

That weekend was horrendous. I kept my mouth shut about the bishop's plans, but in the early afternoon, Pat Zumbolo called again. I guess the others always put Pat up to calling me whenever they were upset with me about something, because they knew, that like Saint Peter, he would just blurt out whatever was on his mind.

"Okay, Father, what are you keeping from us this time?"

Here we go again, now I know he's heard something this time. "Damn it, Pat, I am going to be very honest with you, but first tell me what you have heard."

"That guy across the river shot his mouth off in his church this morning and even broke down crying. He told the parishioners that the bishop betrayed him. The bishop had promised him that he was going to merge Saint Michael's with Mount Carmel, and that he was going to be the pastor of both parishes. But, instead he is going to merge three parishes and told all the pastors to resign. Is that true, Father?"

"Pat, there is nothing I can tell you now, but by tomorrow I will let you all know."

The next day, first thing, I called the chancery, and told the chancellor what had happened and that my people were livid, and were asking me to tell them what I knew. "Under the circumstances, can I tell them?"

He was very upset with the other pastor, and told me I could tell the parishioners, and then told me that because of what happened Mount Carmel was going to be the lead parish and the operation of both parishes would be handled from Mount Carmel when the merger took place. My people were glad to hear that, even though they were upset when I told them that I would be leaving them. It made sense anyway, since we had a huge parking lot, thanks to the foresight of the old timers in the parish who were shrewd enough to consider that when they donated that big piece of land for the new church years before.

The next few months were a nightmare. It was like a four-month wake. We all decided not to discuss the matter, and to carry on as if nothing happened. There was nothing we could do about it, so we just enjoyed what little time we still had together. Though we never discussed it, it was on everyone's mind, and I could sense they were trying to figure out how I felt. The way they looked at me, told me that they were waiting for me to tell them my feelings. About things like that I was always silent, as difficult as it was for me. It was one of those times when a priest has to be loyal and support his bishop. I kept my feelings to myself. I don't think I even shared it with Gilda. I felt it was cowardly to put the burden on others hearts. I had to process it myself, and prayed over it so I could resolve it in my own soul to the point where I felt at peace.

But, there was something inside me that made me feel very uneasy as if something very ominous was about to happen. I didn't know what it was, but I was beginning to feel frightened about the future. I did not know whom I could trust. I did not feel I could trust my future to the chancery officials. Though the chancery thought otherwise, I was always loyal to the bishop, which he found out later on when the merger actually took place. I had spent six years trying to help the people have a good feeling about the bishop, though that was hard, because I knew how the chancery officials felt about me, and they were not too discreet in keeping it to themselves, which I found out from friends who were close to the chancery officials, some of whom worked there.

In late spring, my family wanted to celebrate Mom and Dad's 50th wedding anniversary. Since there was so much room at the parish, and I wanted the parishioners to be part of it in some way, I pressured my brothers and sisters into having it at a restaurant across the highway from the church, even if it was only for a short time after Mass.

The Mass was heavily attended by the parishioners. My parents had such deep faith, and loved the Church. I owe my love of the Church and my closeness to Jesus to my mother and father, and as I offered a thanksgiving Mass that day for them, I glanced at them every now and then. I could tell they were deep in prayer. Their souls were so intensely bonded to God when they prayed, something I had seen so often when I was a child growing up. The way they prayed was so different. I think my father must have had ecstasies. No one could distract him when he prayed. To see them so deep in prayer at this celebration of their anniversary made me realize that even now as we were all celebrating their lives, they were both absorbed in God. It made me feel so ashamed that I could not be more like them, in the saintly simplicity of their lives. At Communion time, it was an honor to offer them Jesus, and they received Him with such reverence.

After spending time outside under the trees with the parishioners, we went over to the restaurant. The restaurant was owned by parishioners. Since my mother had been suffering from serious heart problems, we had to keep things relatively relaxed. It was a beautiful occasion, and a rare chance for us all to get together and express our gratitude for these two self-sacrificing individuals who dedicated their whole life to us, and made so many good things in life possible for us, especially our faith, which they taught us to focus on Jesus. At the end of the day, my parents went back home and the parish was again quiet.

Chapter Eleven

As July approached, the bishop called and told us that we had to make the announcement that the changes were imminent. I told him that it was not our place to make the announcement. It had to come from those who made the decision. He was concerned about how the people would treat him. I promised him our people would treat him with respect. To give him credit, he announced that he was coming to Amsterdam and would be talking with the parishioners of the three parishes involved.

It took place on a Sunday afternoon and evening. He visited with the people of the three parishes starting with the other two. At Mass that morning, and at the vigil Mass the night before, I spoke to the parishioners about the coming visit, and tried the best I could to show that the decision was necessary and that there would be many more disturbing things in the future as the Church is going through most difficult times. They knew that I had been preparing them since the beginning for disturbing things like this, though, at the time, no one believed me. We had had a good six years and had a lot of fun together as we accomplished so many beautiful things that helped and enabled so many. The bishop never interfered in all the things we were doing. Now was our chance to rise to the occasion and show respect for the bishop who had a most difficult task during very trying times. I expected them to listen to what he would say and be gracious to him. At one of the

Masses, the NBC affiliate from Schenectady came with their cameras and reporters and taped the Mass and the sermon. That was difficult for me, since the talk was very intimate to a parish family with whom I had bonded so warmly. I had to weigh every word so carefully. The television reporter was a nephew of one of the priests who was asked to resign. I could not appear to be a wimp in the face of authority, nor critical of the bishop's decision, and at the same time, show the parishioners my heartfelt concern for them and for their future. I also told them that it is their parish, and that I had trained them to stand firm in difficult times. I knew they would. One thing they knew, and that was that I was loyal to them, and I knew they would be loyal to me when I told them to be gracious toward to bishop.

When the bishop came later, in early evening, he was totally drained. I could tell he was deeply shaken, and told me he had been treated horribly in the other two parishes. I told him he did not have to worry, that our people would treat him with respect, so there was no need to worry.

I did not attend the meeting. He wanted to speak to the people. When he came out, he looked relaxed. He told me how kind our people were toward him, even though he realized how very painful this was for them. And then he said, "Joe, I really owe you for this. How different your people were from the way they treated me in the other parishes." I am sure he meant it.

I don't know just when our resignations were to take effect, and when the new pastor would come, but when it did happen, we left our parishes, and did not know where to go. We had no assignments. One of the three left the diocese for a while, the other left and got a job working in a brickyard. I went home to stay with my parents and told them that I was planning to give them an anniversary present and take them on a month's vacation to the Grand Tetons, in Jackson, Wyoming, which I told them were so beautiful. I did not want them to worry, or worry about how I felt. I was disappointed that I had no assignment, and I called the chancellor and asked when I was going to be assigned and he said I had to let the bishop know what assignment I would like. I told him that there was an opening for a campus minister at Rensselaer Polytechnic Institute, and he told me to apply. I applied and was told that I had to be interviewed by two boards at the college, which I went through. I waited for weeks and heard nothing, for another few weeks and heard nothing. During that time, I helped at the parish where my parents lived. The pastor needed someone to help with Sunday Masses.

Finally, I called the bishop and I asked if he had heard anything. "Oh, they didn't tell you? They said you were too old to work with young people." That hurt. I hope it wasn't intended to hurt. I felt he didn't have to word it that way. I knew I worked well with young people. It showed at Mount Carmel. Then, I decided that since I had no assignment in sight, it would be a good time to take my parents on their vacation which I did every summer anyway. So, we started out for Wyoming. I always loved to drive. It took my mind off things as we immersed ourselves in all the beauties of the wide Western landscapes. This time we took the northern route, going through Canada, and then toward Michigan where we stopped off to visit some friends, the Souliers, on their little farm. I had taught Mary Ann in high school in Pottsville, Pennsylvania, years before, and their whole family remained dear friends through the years. We didn't stay long, just a few hours, then continued on our way.

It took us a little less than four days to reach Jackson Hole. All along the way we had enjoyed each other's company. We always had fun together, the three of us. Dad was fun. He fixed a big Styrofoam picnic box full of steaks, and cold cuts, and beer and soda, and all kinds of goodies. He was great at preparing picnics. All along the way we stayed at motels, and had Mass each morning, most of the time on a picnic table at a roadside park. During the day, we stopped at picnic areas and had the time of our life. That simple meal each night was a high point of the day. I started the fire and then put bacon on the grill, and after a few minutes took it off and made bacon sandwiches which we all loved while the grease from the bacon made a great fire to grill the strip steaks, and fried potatoes and corn. Along the way dad picked up home grown beefsteak tomatoes and sliced them. They were the best dinners on the whole trip, and so much simple fun. My dad had never had vacations most of his life. He worked hard. It was only the last few years after he closed his store that he would come on vacations with Mother and me.

We finally arrived at Jackson Hole and Jackson, and the resort. The view was breathtaking. There were three different sections to the resort. One was specifically for hikers, one for campers, and the main place which also had an area with large, comfortable motel rooms which we had previously arranged for. Not many people knew about this place. It was run by a subsidiary of the Rockefeller Foundation, called Rock Resorts, and was frequented mostly by members of congress and their friends. It was a perfect place for a rest, which I badly needed. Those of us who lived in the motel section had access to the vast sitting room in the main building, which had a huge picture window approximately twenty feet high and even wider, with a breathtaking view of the Grand Teton and Mount Moran. The air was so fresh. The humidity remained at two percent the whole time we were there, except for a rain shower every now and then. The temperature was a constant 84 degrees during the day, but would drop to around 50 at night which was delightful for sleeping. We had arrived there in the afternoon, and had supper at the main building, and then after walking around the grounds we retired for the night.

My mom and dad slept in late. I got up early and walked up a high hill and sat down on a vertical tree trunk and thought, about so many things. I would not let my thoughts dwell on problems. What would I do for the future was my big concern? I knew God wanted me to write about Jesus, and in a way that would make him real for people. It wasn't that I heard voices, but it was like what happened when I was two years old and saw a priest for the first time. I knew that I was supposed to be a priest, and that conviction stayed with me until the first chance I had to go into the seminary, at 14. I had that same understanding, or sense of urgency now, that I was supposed to write, and I knew God wanted me to write about Jesus, because it seemed people can never understand Christianity until they understand Jesus and I had become convinced, through many experiences that even clergy did not know Jesus, even though we talk about him. And it is not just Catholic priests. I found the same thing with ministers, and priests in other churches. I finally realized that it is because seminaries do not teach courses about Jesus that priests treat people according to the law, rather than following the spirit of the Good Shepherd, and focus on the needs of the bruised and hurting sheep. When I wrote and spoke about instituting courses in the seminaries about Jesus, some bishops were offended by my saying that, though there were other bishops who said they would see what they could do to have a course about Jesus put into the curriculum in their diocese. It is only too true that the only courses taught about Jesus are Christology courses, which merely study the development of the doctrines about Jesus the God-Man. That does not teach seminarians about how Jesus thinks and feels and about his struggles and feelings of failure and disappointments and what his attitudes are about so many things, and about all kinds of people. I could never find a book that went that deeply into the interior life of Jesus, and I looked everywhere I could, and read so many books about him, and got so frustrated because scholars seemed so obsessed with just analyzing chapter and verse, and whether individual events or sayings were authentic. It is hard to be drawn to Jesus, and develop a sense of identity with Jesus by reading a life of Jesus by a scripture scholar. In fact, one very famous scripture scholar whom I may have already mentioned who was an advisor on scripture to Pope Paul VI told me much later on, shortly after I had finally written "Joshua," that he read "Joshua" every morning, together with the gospels, because it told him so much about Jesus that fed him spiritually. And before he died, he had read "Joshua" close to fifteen times.

During those thirty days in the mountain, I spent the time thinking and listening, listening to a very quiet voice inside, nudging me, guiding me, comforting me, each morning up in that little hill while waiting for my parents to rise and ready themselves for Mass. It is surprising how easy it is to sense the delicate presence of God when the soul is quiet, and far from the turmoil of the busy world. Each day I felt a stronger urgency to write, and I knew I was not responding. I always found it difficult to write. There was a psychological block. I never looked upon myself as a writer, and knew that if I wrote there would be no style to it. One newspaper editor said that my writing was boring and uninteresting. And that was the editor for Carl Bernstein and Bob Woodward. That was a difficult obstacle for me to overcome. It was only when I had to write the Human Rights Commission reports that I finally realized the power of truth and honesty in appealing to the public. It convinced me that people were not negative about changes in society, but are very positive and supportive when injustice is presented in a way that was not radical, and when facts were presented in an objective and honest fashion.

I had found the same response to my weekly letters in the parish bulletin, and how positive the people were even though they may not have attended Mass every week. I was beginning to feel very strongly about what seemed to be needed in Christianity, and that was a renewal of knowledge and interest in Jesus. The one thing I had been afraid of in becoming pastor was that I knew if I followed my conscience in guiding the people I was going to have problems, because of my attitude that I must try to be a good shepherd like Jesus, and put the needs of the sheep first. It was not prudent for the bishop to appoint me to be pastor, as I knew I would cause trouble and it pained me to be in a predicament that made me feel so uncomfortable. My superiors in the monastery gave me difficult assignments because they knew I would give it my best shot, and usually do well in trying. But, being pastor was a veritable nightmare. I had tried to explain to the personnel director, when I was first asked, though my objections were overruled.

The problem I was beginning to understand comes from deep within me, and about an area of my life that I had never allowed myself to analyze because it I was afraid of where it might lead. Now I could no longer repress it. It was clear to me that Christianity and the way it was taught to people was flawed, dangerously flawed, and turning people, especially young people away from the Church. This does not mean that the Church had stopped teaching the truths of Jesus' message, but that the truths were taught and the laws were made without reference to the Person of Jesus, but what was good for the Church. And it wasn't just the Catholic Church. The administration of the churches of all denominations had made the same mistake. We had lost sight of the real message of Christianity, and have made the medium of the message, the message. Jesus is the religion. He is the message. The Church is the medium of the message. The Bible is the medium of the message. When the apostles went out to spread the gospel, they did not teach theology. There was no theology developed yet. They did not teach the Church, except to say it was the mystical body of Jesus, and as such it was sacred as the bride of Christ. It was one with Jesus and was composed of all those baptized into Jesus who believed all that Jesus taught. Nor did the apostles preach bible, especially to pagans; to Jews, yes, as Jesus was the fulfillment of their prophecies, so those who were preaching to the Jews were heavy into the Jewish scriptures. But to the Greeks and others the Bible as yet had no relevance. They did not preach the New Testament, as there was no New Testament yet. They preached Jesus as their message. "Let me tell you about my friend Jesus," and they went on to tell the whole story of Jesus and his life, death and resurrection, and that he is the Savior of the whole human race, and in following him faithfully, we can be born again into God's family, and would one day live forever with him in paradise. For centuries Jesus was the focus of Christianity. Even though there were bad Christians, even bad leaders, noxious weeds in this vast field of wheat, there were also, at the same time, many beautiful and glorious saints living heroically Christ-like lives through every age of history and throughout the whole Church.

However, even though the so-called Reformation was a wakeup call to the Catholic hierarchy, it did a great disservice to Jesus by forcing him into the background, and tearing apart the Mystical Body of Christ, torching Europe with Christian wars for over a hundred years. As denominations began to proliferate, princes ordered the subjects to become followers of Luther or Calvin by threatening execution or confiscation of property. In this way, the local lords could have total control over their people, and be free from foreign domination by the Holy Roman Emperor, who was at the time, Spanish. The various churches, Catholic and Protestant, then began to produce catechisms, rather than teach Jesus, to promote the teachings of their denominations. These were used to catechize and prepare people for baptism. Jesus was almost universally made secondary to the differing doctrines of each denomination, even though they taught children nice bible stories about the kind and meek and gentle Jesus, the studies never went very deep into an understanding of what was important to Jesus. And after all these centuries that have passed, what is taught today about Jesus in seminaries is skimpy, covering merely the development of the doctrines about Jesus as the God-Man. In some Protestant seminaries, even this course in merely an elective, which means that those who elect not to take that course will never have a clear cut understanding of the Person of Jesus, and whether he is human, divine, or a melding of the two natures, and whether he was always God, or only later became a god as some religions teach. But there are no courses which try to plumb the depths of Jesus' thinking about so many real-life situations, especially the dramatic difference between the scribes and Pharisees and Jesus as the Good Shepherd. When Jesus described the Good Shepherd, his description was totally opposite to the ways of the Pharisees and the way they treated people who could not measure up to the laws. The Pharisees had a thousand reasons for excommunicating people, and cutting them off from God. Jesus, when he describes the good shepherd, he paints him as a shepherd who goes out looking for those the Pharisees excommunicated: the hurt, the bruised, the damaged sheep, the lost, and when he finds them, he picks them up, places them on his shoulders and carries them back home. The Pharisees hated Jesus for showing love and acceptance of those people they expelled from the temple and the synagogue.

Now what happens in Christian churches? What model do we follow? I gave a talk down south a while back. After the talk, a lady who told me she was Southern Baptist, came up to tell me about her daughter. The daughter's husband left her and got a divorce. The next Sunday when the daughter went to church, two of the ushers came to where she was sitting and told her to stand up. They then told her that she was no longer a member of the

155

congregation since is divorced, and they proceeded to lead her out of the church and told her she was no longer welcome. The poor woman was devastated and so was the mother.

And there are similar problems in other denominations as well. In practically every Catholic parish perhaps 40 percent of the parishioners are divorced and remarried without the Church's blessing. They are told that they still should attend Mass but cannot receive Communion. They are considered unworthy to receive Jesus' embrace. Yet, we allow unjust judges and lawyers and other professional people, as well as all kinds of other sinners, to receive Communion to the scandal of parishioners who know all these people. Something is wrong. The Pharisees kicked sinners out of the religion. The Good Shepherd goes out and tries to find them, the bruised, the hurting, the troubled sheep, and carries them back home because he loves the sheep. And when he gets them back home, would he say to them, "Now you go in the corner there while the rest of us have supper?" It is so unChristlike. If we insisted on all those people applying and receiving annulments first before they remarry, it would take God knows how many years for, say 15,000,000 American Catholics alone, to be processed for annulments. It does not even make sense. To give Pope Benedict credit, he at least raised the issue and asked the bishops to reconsider the law refusing Communion to people who are divorced and remarried without the Church's blessing. He is trying, but now he is stuck with overly conservative bishops whom he himself appointed, and made it clear the Vatican must decentralize and let bishops share in the decision-making process. I wonder how he will resolve this conflict.

But, the example of Jesus is clear. If Jesus goes out of his way to embrace sinners, who are we to say that sinners cannot come and allow Jesus to embrace them. That is Jesus' business. It is interesting that at the Last Supper, Jesus did not wait until Judas left before he gave the apostles his body and blood as the food of their souls. He gave them the Eucharist while Judas was still present. How tender, as one last expression of his love and attempt to touch his heart. And he knew that Judas was already in the state of mortal sin as we would say, for having made the commitment to betray Jesus. How theologically incorrect, one might say today, except it was Jesus doing it! Something is tragically wrong with our approach, and denying Communion to people whom canon law said was forbidden, was one of the most difficult problems for me when I was pastor. Whenever I asked myself what would the Good Shepherd do when it came to giving Communion to people who were in violation of the law, one thing was very clear, I could never imagine him saying to someone who came to him hurting, "Leave me. You are not worthy to embrace me. If Jesus did not say no to Judas, who then should ever be turned away. I never wanted it on my conscience when I appeared before God that I refused to let Jesus embrace someone who was reaching out to him for hope and comfort, especially in times of desperation. It would haunt me to think that I was sending that person back to the darkness of their tortured life with the terrible guilt that they were cut off from God. Jesus never treated sinners that way. Nor could I.

These experiences convinced me that we Christians do not know the real Jesus, and we model God after our own attitudes, to make him think like we think, so we rarely feel a need to change and do things differently. I began to realize that I had come so far away from all I had been taught, it frightened me. In my struggling through the gospels, and in my prayer life which I had learned as a Carmelite a different Jesus became so vivid and so real in my mind and in my heart, that it changed the whole way I looked on what our faith should mean to us in real life and in the way we treat people. I now realized that I had become an oddity to others, and a troublemaker, which I never intended to be. Then it dawned on me that they did not see the same Jesus that I had come to know through all the pain and torture of my life. I now knew very clearly that I was supposed to share this Jesus with the world, whether I was right or wrong.

Chapter Twelve

In the quiet, peaceful days on the mountain in Wyoming, my whole life passed before me, and I finally saw what it was all about. My not going to Rome as a young theology student, now seemed a blessing, and my seemingly senseless assignments were not haphazard, or arbitrary decisions of an uncaring God, but a very carefully planned strategy so that I would have all the experiences I needed to see Jesus in all levels of society, and among all kinds of people, from people with highest honors, to ordinary people struggling to live reasonably. I need to see Jesus in the forgotten criminals wasting away in prisons as outcasts of humanity, and to the forgotten and those considered useless and the scum of society. And along side of that was close association with people of all different faiths, Christian, Jewish, Buddhist, Hindus. At those times as I was passing through all those experiences I could not understand what was happening, as the parade of seemingly disconnected experiences made no sense to me. Other priests' lives seemed to be so orderly and so well organized. I envied them. Why can't I be like that, so that my superiors can see me as a sensible hardworking priest with something to offer? Instead, I was a troublemaker and a malcontent, and insubordinate. How many times my pillow was wet from my tears! I knew I was an oddity, an enigma, whose life was out of control, and there seemed to be nothing that I could do to change it.

Now I knew. All those experiences were not haphazard, but absolutely necessary for me to see Jesus in every aspect of human life, and how he would respond to the needs of God's children in all those varied situations of human life at all levels of society.

The pressure on me now was a sharp pain driving me to write about this Jesus whom I had come to know. That need that I had resisted for so long was now a sharp pang of conscience that was becoming more uncomfortable with each passing day. I knew I had to do it. But, how do I start?

The peace on the mountain was a two-edged knife. I saw things clearly which brought resolution and serenity, but also pain and fear at the realization that I had to write about something so difficult as a different understanding of Jesus, and all the added misunderstanding and alienation it will bring. Will it never end? While up in the mountain each morning, facing that awesome Mount Moran which was so overwhelming it seemed only a few feet away, and it was peaceful. God was there in the silence and in the cool morning breeze, and though I was alone, I felt at peace. I did feel sadness because I knew I could never be accepted by those for whom I had the highest regard. To many priests I was a stranger known only by the rumors that circulated, though some were kind to me. I don't think there was a time in my life that I ever felt more alone, yet the presence of God was never more comforting.

Our daily Mass in the motel room was a deeply spiritual experience for me and my parents. Their piety as they prayed with me always made me feel unworthy. They were authentically holy. I only could wish I was holy. I could never feel I was holy. All I could feel was that I was a disappointment to God. The presence of Jesus in the room with us created such a beautiful bond, and my prayer every day was a soulful plea, "God, please make me a good priest." That was all I ever wanted, all I ever prayed for. It is still after all these years my constant prayer. Everything else is irrelevant, for from the heart of a good priest all Jesus' graces flow into the lives and hearts of others. To both my parents I seemed to be at peace, as I never wanted them to think I was in pain. That would hurt them too much. I don't think I shared anything with them. It was their anniversary, so well-earned after raising the 12 of us, who had already given them so much worry and anxiety. What made me happy was I was finally able to see my mom and dad being affectionate with each other. All their lives they had always been highly disciplined and reserved in their show of affection for each other. Now, away from everybody and everything familiar they were like a young couple on a date. I made believe I wasn't noticing, so they would feel free to enjoy their tender moments without someone watching. It was so beautiful and made me feel happy for them. And they were like that for the whole month. It was like a honeymoon after 50 years of hard labor.

Our breakfasts we enjoyed in the main building, while enjoying the vision of the mountain and the lake spread out at its base where moose grazed every morning. Occasionally a huge bull moose with gigantic antlers would wander closer to the building so we could get an exciting glimpse of those magnificent animals. Breakfast was always fun. Mom and dad looked so rested and relaxed. We reminisced about the past, and what we were all like when we were kids. My mother reminded me that even when I was a child, she could never find me. I always managed to slip out of the house and wander around the neighborhood. I was only about four when the lady upstairs, Susie Delaney, came to the house and told my mother that she had seen me down the street. My mother wouldn't believe her.

"He's sound asleep in bed, Susie, I'll show you." When she showed her friend the bed, she said, "See, Susie."

"Margaret, pull down the covers."

When she did, she saw the pillow under the covers. "That little devil! He must have climbed out the window. But, how could he? He's only four years old."

I don't know how many times she reminded me of that story. Now she could laugh, but it wasn't funny way back them. The kids were their life and their joy, and she was telling me all about each of my brothers and sisters, most of whom grew up while I was away in the seminary for so many years, and later as a priest assigned to areas far from home, so I really didn't know them, though I always had a very tender love for each of them. My affection for them grew as mom described each one's life to me. Dad said very little,

162

other than quaint little comments about the good traits in each of them. They enjoyed telling me all the stories and I enjoyed getting to know my brothers and sisters. I knew they were enjoying their time away. We had always gone on vacation together every summer, though it was only of late that dad would come, when he finally retired. They were treasured times, and something we would continue until they became too frail and needed to be closer to home.

One of the things I could share with my father was my concerns about the Church and how I felt the Vatican was not meeting the needs of the people. He was always very conservative, and both he and mother brought us up to have respect for the Church as Jesus gift to us. Loyalty to the Church was loyalty to Jesus. As big as the Church was, he saw it as a family. When I would comment about needed changes, he would say, "Where, what country?"

I would say, "Well, in the United States for example."

"That's one country. What change do you think the Church should make?"

"Well, about artificial birth control."

"Why, because Americans want it?"

"The Church is more than just Americans."

"Remember when those Indian engineers came to visit, and we were talking about the Church in India, and how shocked Indian

Catholics were about Americans demanding that the Church approve birth control?"

"Yes, I remember that."

"So, there are many good Catholics who do not want the Church to approve of it. One thing about the Church that is very important. It does not cave in to changing moral fashions of the people. It is the shepherd. A shepherd leads. He doesn't follow. The father of a big family has to consider what is good for the family, not what individual children demand."

"Well, dad, wouldn't it have been better on you and mother if the Church changed its rules on birth control? Or would you have been upset with the Church?"

"We would not have been upset with the Church if it changed its attitude. Jesus gave Peter the authority to make laws and change laws, and that authority has been passed on to each pope. When it comes to our family, we did not have children because we had to. We always wanted a big family, and each one of you is precious to us. You will always be our treasure, the only treasure we can bring to heaven when we die. Everything else we have to leave here. Remember, the Church is not a little corner store, or a chain of supermarkets where people can pick and choose what they want. As God's family, it embraces not just a few countries. It embraces the whole world, and has to care for everybody, all nationalities and people of all cultures."

I was moved at the beauty of such theology. My father could tell he was getting his point across, in his to the point blunt way, so he nicely changed the subject, and suggested we take a ride up into the mountains. My father's thoughts about the Church over the years embraced a wide range of theological concepts about the Church. It was beautiful, especially for a man who had only a sixth grade education. The rest of his education was the fruit of a very contemplative prayer life. I guess that was why some priests used to go to him for counseling when they had difficult problems, and why one bishop attributed his cure of throat cancer to "Peter's prayers," as he told priests who were friends of my father. My mother often just listened, occasionally reminding him, "Don't forgot, you weren't always holy, until I told you had to go to church if you wanted me to marry you."

Never lost for a comeback, my father just said, with good humor, "Why do you think I married you? You were my margarita, my pearl of great price, God's gift."

Sometimes I think my mother was more of a saint than my father, not the least for putting up with him. He could be unbending. Her love of Jesus and the Blessed Mother was so tender. She taught us all our prayers, kneeling down with us each night, teaching us how to pray and talk to God, and saying our prayers with us. Her faith was deep and quiet, and expressed not much in words, but in the beauty of her life, and the way she talked to us, as if the spiritual world was just as real as the world around us. It was her prayers said for us when she knew we were hurting or troubled. We never had to tell her. She knew, and what was so remarkable, she never pried or asked us if everything was okay. She just prayed her prayers of quiet desperation for each of the 12 of us when she knew something was not right. How we knew was when she would casually tell one of us that she was praying for us special. That's all she would say, other than just, "Trust God and the Blessed Mother, and don't be afraid. Everything eventually works out." Then we knew she knew whatever it was, but she never pried.

While we were staying at the Tetons, we took many side trips. One of them was to Jackson Lake on the western side of the Tetons. We just drove along that clear fresh water on our way to Yellowstone National Park, which was not very far, just a day trip from Jackson. Of course, Old Faithful was the awesome site, always spraying high into the air, and always precisely on schedule. The pools of boiling water were an impressive experience, knowing that that water bubbled up from deep beneath the surface of the earth. There was nothing to do there but just stand there and think about nature's wonders. After driving around through the park we started back to Jackson, enjoying the fresh mountain air. How peaceful and quiet! Dad sat in the back seat and made sandwiches along the way. He was good at that, especially for the slices of delicious homegrown tomatoes he picked up as we shopped along the way, and which he put in the sandwiches. As proper as he always was with us as we were growing up, the child in him came out in so many ways during the long trip. He saw and experienced everything as if through the eyes of a child who was seeing life for the first time. His observations were so revealing of things most of us would overlook in God's creation. He saw everything in nature as related, and dependent on each other. What a remarkable first principle for respecting the environment!

One of the nice things about extended vacations like that one was the variety of places where we ate. At the park, there were three choices, the main building, which was plush and more formal, then the one at Jenny Lake, which was for the hikers, and which we didn't visit, and the one at Coulter Bay, which was for campers, and mobile homers, where there was a classy restaurant, very airy, with a relaxed atmosphere and a big salad bar which was my father's delight. After placing our order, we went to the salad bar. My father was like a little kid at Christmas. He had a wonderful time at the salad bar, filling his plate with all the things he loved and never had at one meal. My mother ate very little and usually ordered fillet of sole, or a light chicken dish, together with what little light salad she put together at the salad bar. I rarely ate lunch, and had just a salad, with olives and tomatoes and olive oil. I would rather have a good supper. When my father's chicken came out, he immediately had it put in a container to take 'home' with him. I asked him, "Dad, what's that all about?"

"That's my supper. How much can I eat at one meal? I had my lunch from the salad bar. The chicken will be my supper."

And he meant it. Later when we were getting ready for supper, he said well, you two can go and waste your money, I got my supper right here," as he took his chicken out of the refrigerator, and started putting his own supper together. We left and went back to Coulter Bay and had a relaxed supper, just mother and I. We spent half the ride to the restaurant talking about dad. "Your father is no different now than when I first met him. He knew as soon as we went into that restaurant that he was going to get two meals out of that luncheon. I could see it when he spotted that salad bar. He's like a little kid. He's always been like that. I suppose it was because things were so hard during the depression. You never get that experience out of your system."

"It does make sense, mom. I just enjoy watching him, and trying to understand the way his mind works. It's all a new experience for me."

"Don't even try. You will never be able to understand him. After 50 years, I still don't know him any better now than I did when I first met him. When we look at something, we see what's there. When he sees something, he sees what it means, and has to understand why?" How do you hold a conversation with a person who thinks at a level you can't even understand? You end up just listening and enjoying because it does make sense."

"But, mother, he's funny, even though he's different. He gets more out of life than most people, and he sees humor in the simplest things, like the time we were coming out of the cemetery and the cars kept driving past the exit and we had a hard time pulling out into the highway. I made the remark they should put a traffic light there. And all Dad said was, 'There's not too many coming out of here.' I laughed so hard at his rapid-fire response. He had already thought what I had been thinking, but went a step further and figured out why they never put a traffic light there. You can have a lot of fun with him. He's a good companion."

"He is, but that's because he's not under pressure now that the kids are all grown up. With 12 kids to worry about, there wasn't much fun. It was too stressful to have fun. The most fun we had was just enjoying all of you, and watching you all grow up. You were all so different, and so full of energy. I could never understand how your father could fall asleep at the table after eating his dinner. He would fall sound asleep holding the newspaper up as if he was reading it, and yet you knew he was sound asleep, even with all the noise from twelve kids."

"I remember that, and then one of us would start yelling at somebody, and daddy would yell out, 'All right, once more and you go to bed,' and I would look at him and he was still asleep, still holding up the newspaper. It was weird. I guess he was really tired, after a hard day. But, mother, you couldn't afford to get tired. After daddy went to bed, you still had to stay up and do the ironing."

"That was the most peaceful time of the day for me, and you usually stayed up to help me, and I'd send you down to Henny Murphy's before he closed, to get milk or bread, and a popcorn square and a maple bell, which we'd split when you came back. You were my companion then. It was hard when you left at 14 and went into the seminary. But, I knew you had to go. You told me when you were two years old, after church one Sunday that you were going to be a priest. That was so painful. I knew I would lose you forever."

"And here we are, mother, just like old times, and even with dad enjoying the fun with us. It was not easy, mother, being a priest. If I could only be like other priests!"

"You're a lot like your father. You keep everything locked up inside. Isn't it difficult not sharing it with anybody?"

"Sharing what, mother?"

"See, you won't even open the door."

"Mother, how can I share what I don't even understand myself? I am at peace. When I'm troubled, I walk in the woods and feel close to God and to Jesus, and I know they are with me, and if they are close, I feel at peace. Don't worry, mother, nothing will ever drive me off course. I am very close to God, and knowing that he's near, what does anything else matter? But, I'm glad we had a chance to talk like this. My life as a priest has been beautiful, mother, and the problems are not insurmountable. They just make us stronger. It no different than being married, so don't worry about me, mother, I am still tough, just like I was when I was a kid'

"And you were that all right. But, you always did have a kind heart."

It was getting dark and it was chilly outside the restaurant. When we got back to the motel, dad was sound asleep. It was a happy day, and a rare night when my mother and I had one of the nicest talks we've had since I was 12 years old and used to help her when everyone else went to bed. As way back then, so this time, she shared with me things that were on her mind, and her concern for each of us. What a mother!

Early the next morning I went back up on the hill, and started to write. I know it was not about Jesus, though I cannot remember what I was writing about. It has totally escaped me. It must have been the beginning of one of my books, probably "Who Will Teach Me?" a handbook for parents to teach their own children about their faith. I also recall wandering around just for the sheer enjoyment. The air was fresh and clean and so healthy especially at that time of the day, and there was not a sound, no motors, no horns, just a gentle breeze through the tall grass, and an occasional calling of a bird or an animal of some sort, or the shriek of a hawk as it glided along an air current, or the powerful bellow of a moose.

Mom and dad were getting used to the high elevation, over 6,000 feet, and the thin amount of oxygen. I was a little worried about mother, because her heart was weak, but as long as she rested enough, she seemed to be all right. When I asked her how she felt, she seemed totally unconcerned and said she had no symptoms of any trouble, though she noticed she did get tired

171

towards early afternoon. So, we started taking a rest at that time. We all needed it.

One day, while we were all resting, dad snored like something you would hear in the middle of a jungle. He would never admit that he snored, so this time I decided to record it. I was delighted it turned out so well, so when he woke up, I played the recording. He very calmly said, "What's that?"

I said, "It's you snoring."

"That's no proof. That could be anybody. There's no way you can prove to me that I snore. Even if you told me your mother is a witness. I would consider the two of you biased, and not credible witnesses."

He wriggled out of that too easily. I have never been able to develop a way of convincing him that he snored, and he went to his grave, I think, knowing he had outfoxed us right to the end.

Only one other time I thought I had him, when he was in a deep sleep and suddenly snored real loud, and woke himself up. So, I knew I had him.

"Well, dad, your snoring finally even woke you up, you were snoring so loud."

"It wasn't snoring that did it, it was you two plotting that frightened me. I knew you were up to something."

I finally gave up. It was impossible to outfox him. I would have loved to have seen him on a witness stand being cross examined by lawyers. His responses, I am sure, would have been priceless.

At one of the meals in the main building, it was announced that there was going to be a raft ride down the Snake River, and that the group will meet at the dock at 4:30 the next morning. We decided to do it.

Dad woke up automatically at 3:30. I could never figure out how he could do that without an alarm clock. During his whole life he woke up at precisely the time he decided to wake up, and without an alarm. We met the others at the dock, and promptly at 4:30 the rafts, each one holding about eight people, took off and started drifting down the river on the rapid current. There was not a sound, and no sooner had we started the trip than animals and ducks and birds appeared along the river looking for their breakfast. There were species of ducks I had never seen before. Their strange antics were so funny, all of us in the raft were laughing at the show, which to us was so ridiculously humorous, but to the ducks it was their serious lovemaking ritual. Maybe it was just God's sense of humor, to make us serious humans laugh.

The trip was an eye-opening experience for all of us, seeing all the animals, hundreds of species that depend on the river each day for sustenance. It was one of the most fascinating experiences we have ever encountered, and would never forget all that we had seen. If we had wandered through the forests for years we would

173

never have encountered the display of varied species that we saw on that ten-mile raft ride down the Snake River. The ride took two hours and when we arrived at our destination, we disembarked and went to a delightful little restaurant for breakfast, then were taken back to the lodge by bus. It was a real fun trip, and when we got to the motel, the three of us were ready for a nap.

The four weeks went fast, and though we could have stayed for another month it was so relaxing, the weather started to change as August was approaching. From August on, the winter begins and soon the whole place pretty well closes down. When the snow starts in August or September, eventually the whole resort becomes totally snowed in. It was time to start our long journey back home.

Chapter Thirteen

The ride back home was relaxed and easy. The first place we stopped was at Custer National Park to wander through the site of the Battle of the Little Big Horn. As we read the story of what happened there, it was so clear that it was tragic for both sides, and so unnecessary, such a waste of human life. Of course, we were innocent as we always are in the eyes of super patriots for whom their country can do no wrong. But, this time the Indians were wise to General Custer and outmanned and out maneuvered him and ended up killing him there. While in the area, in the Crow Reservation, we went to Mass on Saturday night at a small church along the way. At the offertory time, I struggled with how generous I should be in the collection. I wrestled with myself longer than I should have, but decided that God had been so good to us and realized that I had spent so much on ourselves, I should also be generous in thanking God. I finally decided to make a generous donation. I am so glad I did. My Dad always said, "You cannot outdo God in generosity."

The next day we left the reservation, and near the exit next to the Crow Agency Headquarters we passed a gas station, with a big sign in front, "Next gas station 400 miles. So I filled up the tank, and took off. Hardly three miles down the road, the air conditioner stopped working. Dad said, "That's a warning. You better go back and have the man check it. It could be a broken fan belt and if that's the problem, we're going to have serious trouble. We could even burn out the engine. So, I reluctantly went back to the station, and talked to the attendant. He said "The mechanic shop is closed, but, the mechanic is in there working on his own car. You might talk to him and see if he wouldn't mind helping you."

I went inside and apologized to the mechanic for interrupting him on his day off. The man was very kind. He lifted up the hood of the car and looked at the engine and said that one of the fan belts broke and fell off. He looked to see if he had a replacement for the one our car needed. He had none, but said he would see if there was another brand that could do the job. Fortunately, he found the only one left, and in five minutes installed it, and sent us on our way. He charged only cost but I was so appreciative, what extra I gave him was well worth it. He told us that if we had continued on our way, the engine would have burnt out and we would have had to have the car towed for almost four hundred miles, which they would not have been able to do until Monday, two days away. That meant that we would have had to spend the night in a desolate place that was full of rattlesnakes, especially at night, and the searing heat. That would have been tragic. Just thinking of the cost of the towing, and the cost of a new engine, and the delay while waiting for the engine to arrive, and the cost of the motel for at least two nights, and the danger to mom with her bad heart, being stuck out in that terrible heat. I could not help but think that God had already rewarded us for that extra gift in the collection at Mass the night before. You cannot outdo God in generosity."

We traveled only about 600 miles each day, with a number of convenient breaks, and had supper at very interesting restaurants along the way. The one my father liked the most was in Minnesota, out in cattle country. The sign outside, which read, "Grill your own steaks," appealed to dad as a meat cutter. "Let's stop in there. That looks like a nice place." So, there we stopped. Once inside we saw tables spread out across the huge space, and along the wall a whole row of gas grills, where the customers could grill their own steaks just the way they wanted them. Grilling your own steak right in the middle of cattle country, what more could a butcher want. Best thing next to heaven. Dad always told his customers that he had only corn-fed western steer. It was his big boast, plus the fact that his meat was from the only place that had federal inspectors. As his steak was cooking, the owner walked past and my father started a conversation with him. "This is a great idea you have, each one cooking his own steak."

"Yes, the customers love it."

Then my father asked him the fatal question, "Where do you get the beef from?" knowing he was going to say they were local corn-fed steer. But, that was not it. He said, "We get our beef from Pittsburgh, and then realized that that did not sound quite right, so he immediately added, "but it is raised here and then shipped to Pittsburgh to be cut up and packaged. It is then sent back out here."

After that my father said merely, "Well, you can tell it is western corn-fed meat," hoping that the man was telling the truth.

"That it is," the man agreed.

My father really enjoyed that steak. I am sure he dreamed about it more than once after he got back home, and couldn't wait to tell his friends about that restaurant where you grill your own steaks, all western corn-fed beef, of course. But, he never said it came from Pittsburgh.

After that dinner, which was a mini-climax of the trip for dad, the journey home was uneventful, except maybe for a side trip in Illinois, where we had stopped once before outside of Springfield, to visit the log cabin village out in the woods, where Abraham Lincoln lived when he practiced as a lawyer. This tiny village is kept in remarkable condition and shows how simply this great man lived before he became president. There were nice houses out in that area, but he didn't live in one until much later. That place is in the city of Springfield itself. But, this log cabin village outside of Springfield tells much about Lincoln without a word being said. Just to stand there on that dirt street and meditate on what life must have been like for him, tells a biography without words, a life story in itself. On one occasion when we were there, a concert was given in a good size natural amphitheater on the site of the modest village, a concert consisting of period instruments, and period music, probably the kind of concert people played at that time to entertain the simple folk of that day.

I don't remember whether we really did stop there this time on our way back home, or did we just reminisce over times we did, and relived the experience since we were driving not very far from the place, just south of Chicago. We were now on the direct line for home and were in a hurry to get back and get settled again. The time went fast, and if I remember correctly we finally reached home late Wednesday afternoon, glad to see everybody who missed mother and dad, who had never been away from their brood for such a long period of time. They were given a very warm welcome which touched them deeply.

It took a few days to get back in shape after all the driving. Surprisingly none of us gained any weight after that whole month of relaxing. We did walk a lot and wander around, just enjoying the scenery. I took some pictures of the Tetons from different angles so I could paint a picture with a 3-D feeling when I got back home, and strangely enough, now if you stand back more than 12 feet from the painting, you get the illusion of three dimensions. I still don't understand how it works on the mind.

"We always hoped that Jesus would be the way you presented him in your talk, but we never heard anybody talk about Jesus like that, and it is so healing."

Chapter Fourteen

After a few days home, and still no calls from the bishop, I did not know what to think. Could it be that I had given the chancery such a difficult time, that they were hoping I would just go away? The previous bishop had said as much to my Carmelite friends while visiting them, telling them he wished he could get rid of me. It was already three months and I still had no assignment and no one seemed interested in giving me one. People from my old parish, Mount Carmel, wrote and called to tell me the new priest had changed everything, had painted over the paintings in the chapel, had taken down the tabernacle and put the old one back, and had taken all the keys back and told the people they were going back to the old ways. That nice pastoral letter the bishop had written was just propaganda, as far as they were concerned. He also withdrew sponsorship of the Office on Aging, which was picked up by Saint Mary's Hospital. I tried to calm them down and remind them that I changed everything when I went there, so each pastor has his own ideas as to how he sees things, so just get him into dialoguing with the parishioners and in time things will work out. It had always been my policy never to become involved in a parish that I had left, and I strictly stuck to that.

Still not having an assignment, my fear had finally come true. They could care less if I ever got an assignment. I finally called the bishop's office and, I admit I was not nice. I told him bluntly, "After all this time I still don't have an assignment, and I feel that I can no longer in conscience allow my life to be controlled by incompetent people."

A few days later the bishop did call to tell me that there was a parish vacant, but 13 priests had already applied for it, and though he was reluctant to give it to me because he felt I had psychological problems, he told me that if I wanted it, he would take a chance and give me the assignment. I accepted, and went down to Saint Patrick's Church in Ravena, New York, at the beginning of September, 1978.

It was a quaint, very old parish with a small church building reminiscent of an English village church, made of brick, with a slate roof. Inside, rafters and beams held up the slate roof, but there was no insulation in the roof. The interior walls, were painted a ghostly white, which did not present a warm, prayerful atmosphere, conducive to quiet meditation or prayer.

I went down into the cellar and heard water trickling. Turning on the light I saw a stream flowing in from a spring in the back of the cellar, past the furnace and down the length of the cellar where it finally disappeared somewhere. In times of heavy rain, I later found out, the stream went right through the base of the furnace, flooding it, and shutting off the heat. I isolated the furnace from the floor around it and secured it from the stream by a concrete wall. That was my first problem, not a big problem, just a mysterious one.

The people in the parish were nice people from what I could see on first contact. They seemed accepting of me. The previous pastor, they told me, was very conservative and old school. On the previous Christmas, there was a blizzard on Christmas Eve, and by morning the snow was 15 inches deep, so deep the plow drivers could not get from their houses to the plows, so none of the streets were plowed, and only a handful of devoted parishioners made it to Mass. "Most of us were in our 70s and 80s, and happy we were able to make it to church," a lady told me. "When the priest rose to deliver the sermon, we could not believe what he talked about. It was a sermon on abortion, wondering what would have happened if Mary chose not to have her child."

Fortunately, the former pastor had already moved out by the time I arrived. There was, however, another priest there, a priest I had been stationed with in Schenectady, New York, nine years earlier. He was a simple fellow, in his 40s, but old fashioned. He had grown up in an Italian neighborhood on Long Island and he would have been happy if he could play Italian music on his accordion all day long for the parishioners. He had been counting on becoming pastor, succeeding the previous pastor. Assured of that, he and a religious sister living at home with her sick parents had already made arrangements with a religious order of brothers to reopen the school which had been closed. It was a bit delicate, and I tried to side step it, hoping the issue would resolve itself. I thought I could count on him being gracious, since I had got myself into so much trouble fighting for him against the pastor in the parish where we had previously worked together.

My first week in the parish I felt a warm welcome from the parishioners. They wished me well when I met them on the street and at the back of church after the weekend Masses. The people were most friendly. The parish secretary was very helpful in familiarizing me with the names of key people in the parish. The two parish trustees were Dr. Robert Whalen, the New York State Health Commissioner, and Jimmy Frangella, who had founded the Frangella Mushroom business, located at the outskirts of the village, and which at that point was still in operation. John Biscone, was the parish lawyer, and one of his sons, John, was the Town Supervisor. The religious education director of the parish was Sr. Biscone, the parish lawyer's sister, and the other priest's friend. Pat Downes was the head of the parish finance committee and the chairman of the town zoning board.

I soon met them all and they were all friendly, and assured me of their help and cooperation. Within a few weeks I became friends with their families, as well as key people in the parish. It took only a short while to understand the composition of the parish. It was an old parish with a complex mix of nationalities, and backgrounds. My previous parish was composed of Italians and Polish or Irish married to Italians, plus others who were longtime friends of Italian families in the parish.

Saint Patrick's was composed of many nationalities, a good number of Italians, but also a large number of Irish, and Germans, as well as Dutch, Belgians, Polish, and some French families, and Walloons. Kitty Mohler was the organist, and a very cultured woman with a doctorate in music. Her husband was Jewish, and a lawyer. Her family was a well-known and widely respected Doyle family from Doylestown, Pennsylvania. There were also some Swiss families in the parish. Politically, the area was predominantly Democrat, but there were also key Republican state officials in the parish. Mary Koechley, the wife of a local dentist, Dr. Bob Koechley, had been a key aide to the Republican Governor Nelson Rockefeller, and had been instrumental in establishing the important academic program for the certification of Social Service professionals. Bob was a most lovable individual and a genuinely holy man, with a great sense of humor, as well as having a reputation for a remarkably adventurous life as a young man. I soon asked if he would be a Eucharistic minister, and in touching humility he felt very honored and was most faithful the whole time I was there.

Joe Frangella, who owned the mushroom plant, was also the County Chairman of the Republican Party. His uncle, Jimmy Frangella, the parish trustee, was a Democrat, as was Dr. Whalen.

There were a number of churches of other denominations in the village, Reverend Joe Ingraham, the pastor of the United Methodist Church, and his wife Mary, became fast friends, and eventually we held Bible Study classes for the people in the area. The other clergy were invited to work with us but declined. Joe surprised me by often showing up at morning weekday Masses to receive Communion.

There also was in the neighborhood an old and highly respected African-American community. They had come north on the underground railroad over 150 years earlier, had settled in Ravena and found work in various places in the area and in the city of Albany, eight miles up the river. They were and still are a remarkable people with a rich and dignified history. They became very dear friends and we shared a lot of laughter and happy times together. I never had such a supportive congregation as I did when I was asked to speak in their church. They sure make a preacher feel proud by the way they voice their loud "Amen, Amen, brother," when the preacher said something they liked. I only wished Catholic people were as encouraging. One family in particular were dear friends; that was the Hughes family. In fact, I just recently visited Jenny Hughes who is now in a nursing home near where I live. When she was younger, and when I was pastor in Ravena, we used to sit on her front porch and chat. They were a beautiful family. Jenny's daughter, and her family were my parishioners. Her sons were the life of the neighborhood.

I also found out later on that there had been at one period of time, a very active Ku Klux Klan, which burned crosses on a field in back of the Catholic Church. I found this out from a former Klan member who had become a dear friend and a very staunch supporter of senior citizen programs I was starting in the community with the generous help of the county Commissioner on Aging. One day, when I was trying to transport a life-size crucifix from the church to the cemetery, I needed a truck. I called a friend who was on my board of directors for Senior Projects in the village. He came with his truck and as we were carrying the crucifix and placing it in the back of his truck, he commented, "If my old Ku Klux Klan friends could only see me now. We used to burn these things out in back of your church. And now the priest is my best friend. How things change!" We both laughed hard at the shocked looks on the faces of neighbors passing by at seeing the two of us together. They all knew him from way back, and were obviously mystified that we could be good friends.

The town itself had a fascinating history. It was built on the western shore of the Hudson River about eight miles south of Albany. It might surprise some people that there are still not just eighteenth century homes along the river in that area and further south, but seventeenth century homes as well. Ravena itself is a village in the town of Coeymans. Coeymans is also the name of a small hamlet right on the river, and adjacent the village of Ravena. The community was originally named after a Dutch landowner, named Barent Pieterse Koijemans, who came over from Holland in 1639, and who later came into possession of a tract of land which was named after him. At the time I was stationed there, a member of the Pillsbury family, of baking products fame, was living in a seventeenth century house on the river in Coeymans.

Not far from the old houses in Coeymans was the Frangella Mushroom farm. It was across the road, and the entrance was perhaps 800 feet from the area of the stately old houses.

It was hardly two weeks into my assignment to the parish when a group of people from the Coeymans' neighborhood asked if they could meet with me. I made arrangements, and as soon as they came to the rectory, they wasted no time in telling me the purpose of the meeting. "Where do you stand regarding the housing project the diocese is planning with the Frangella Mushroom Farm?"

"I have never heard of any such project."

"Don't you sit there and try to tell us that the bishop sent you down here and didn't tell you about the housing project for the migrant workers."

"I am going to be honest with you, I do not know what you are talking about, and I don't care whether you believe me or not. So, if you want to ruin this meeting from the start, keep accusing me of something I know nothing about and we'll get nowhere. If you want to resolve an issue tell me what your problem is, and we'll see how we can resolve it."

The spokeswoman began describing the situation. "The diocese has been planning to build a low-income housing project for the migrant workers at Frangella's mushroom plant. For two years this has been going on behind the backs of the people in the community and the diocese has never approached the town planning board or any of the town officials about what they are doing. The whole community is furious, so we have organized and set up a corporation to fight the bishop. The president of the corporation is Dennis Whalen, Doctor Whalen's son. As you know his father is the State Health Commissioner, and also one of your parish trustees. We also have a war chest to hire a lawyer, and the money for this fund will be coming out of your Sunday collections. Also for your personal information, the town supervisor is the son of your parish lawyer, the head of the zoning board is the chairman of your parish finance committee. Also, it is not just your parishioners who are upset; the local African American community in Coeymans is deeply troubled. These black people in our neighborhood are highly respectable people and have always been dear friends. This housing project will be located right next to where they live. Now, our question is, where do you stand? Whose side are you on, ours or the bishop's?"

I just laughed and said, "You know, I can't believe you people. You hardly even know me and you try to put me in an impossible position like this. I'll tell you what I'll do. I'll find out if what you are saying is true, and if it is, then, out of loyalty to the bishop, who sent me here to be your shepherd and gather this straying flock together, I will have to be on your side and fight the bishop. But, you make it look black and white, when maybe it does not have to be that way. If you people are willing to be part of a committee with diocesan officials, and the diocese is also willing, maybe the joint committee could work together and solve the problem amicably. So, let me do my own research, and talk to the diocese. When I have my answers, I will give you a call and we will set up another meeting. But, one thing I am going to insist on, we are Christians, and we have to have a concern for the poor and the unfortunate. I will not compromise on that, so that has to be basic to all our decisions. If you can agree with me on that now, I will support you." They agreed.

I spent the next few days doing my homework. It was true. The diocese was planning the housing project and it was planned for the area adjacent to the historic homes some of which dated back to the early eighteenth century and a few going as far back as the seventeenth century. Members of the famous Pillsbury family were also opposed to the housing project.

I told the diocese of the situation and asked if they would be willing to work with a committee from the neighborhood. The chancellor, Father Farano, agreed. I also found out from reliable sources that the present owners of the mushroom plant had acquired total ownership from the rest of the family in a way that upset the whole family. Jimmy Frangella, my parish trustee, who had started the business on his own years ago, was now an outsider. I also found out from excellent sources that the plant was in such bad financial shape it would have to file for bankruptcy before long.

I called the spokeswoman for the local committee, and told her that the diocese was willing to work with them. They called the diocese and made plans for their meeting with the diocesan officials. When the meeting took place, the local people were apparently happy with the outcome and come back home in a positive frame of mind. So, the crisis at least seemed to be defused. However, it was not a week later when Dennis Whalen called me from work one morning, and said, in his slow monotone voice, "Well, Father Joe, the chancellor already pulled a fast one on us, and decided without even informing us, much less, consulting us. I am convinced we will not be able to work with these people. They are too devious, and have no intention of letting lay people be part of any decision-making process." I always smiled when Dennis would talk with me. No matter how angry he may be inside, his voice was always perfectly modulated, like a computerized voice with absolutely no show of emotion. But, I knew he was furious. I told him I would consider it and see if I could get them to be more honest and upfront with the committee. We did get back on track, and over a period of time, I could see that it was a waste of time. The diocese had no intention of working with the people. While having supper at Doctor Whalen's house, I asked him how he felt, as a parish trustee, about the project. He was very honest. The project had been poorly planned right from the start. The site is in an area where it will be impossible to get proper facilities, and in that location, water is one of the big problems. The site is badly chosen. Sewage is another big hurdle. There is no way, as the State Health Commissioner, that I could sign a permit approving it. And the fact that the site the diocese chose is right next to all those historic homes, is not helpful at all."

191

With that information, our local committee would have solid ammunition, but I did not think it proper for me to share it with them. I would hold off until the next meeting with the whole committee, and present information I had to the diocese with the whole committee present. That meeting was held a week or two later, if my memory serves me right. At that meeting was the nun who oversaw the project, and top diocesan officials, including their lawyer. Also in attendance were representatives of the Farmers Home Administration, who had agreed to provide financing for the project.

When I got a chance to speak, I merely related what I had found out. "On good authority, I have been told that the mushroom plant is in a very precarious position financially and will probably not be able to survive. If this is true, then for the diocese to go ahead with the project and finish it, they may have no one to live in it, if the migrant workers go back to their own country. Also, the State Health Commissioner stated categorically that there was no way he could give permission for the project, saying that is was poorly planned, that the site they chose was in the wrong place, and that there would be insurmountable health department regulations regarding water and sewage that would make it impossible for the state to approve it.

"However, I would like to suggest for your consideration, a plan that could be approved, and this plan would be certainly acceptable to the people in the village and to the town officials as well. And it would not need town approval. There are a number of blighted houses in the area. And I address this to the representatives of the Farmers Home Administration. Why not go into the village, totally renovate the main street, put up antique style street lamps, antique style signs on the businesses throughout the village, bring all the blighted houses up to code, and also put a small marina down on the waterfront? No one could object to that. The migrant workers could live in those renovated houses scattered throughout the area, and if the mushroom plant should close, and the workers move out, the village will still have newly renovated houses for rent or for sale. I don't think anyone could have a reasonable objection to that, and it would bring peace back to our community."

The Farmers Home people responded very positively to that idea. The diocesan officials said nothing. I could tell they were just waiting for the meeting to end, so they could go back and do whatever they had planned. What I had proposed would not be the subject of controversy, and would be a feather in everyone's cap, to accomplish something so pleasing to a community. Seemingly, although no one told me directly, the plan was acceptable, and plans seemed to be going ahead. The diocese had picked houses which needed renovation, and a problem came up immediately. One of the houses the diocese picked was a two-family house. They decided that they wanted it to be a three-family house, if I am not mistaken. Whatever it was, it entailed having a public hearing with the town officials, which meant it needed zoning board approval, which would be impossible. My plan avoided the issue of town approval. I felt immediately that deep down the diocese did not really want to go along with the plan and this was the way they knew they could scuttle it. Maybe my reasoning was wrong, but I don't think so. The hearing did take place. The afternoon before the meeting that evening, the chancellor called and said that the bishop wanted me to represent him at the hearing and defend the diocese' request for a zoning change. I felt so betrayed, and forced out of loyalty to my bishop, to defend something that I did not believe in. I attended the meeting and tried to make a reasonable defense of the bishop's position, knowing that because of the town officials' resentment toward the diocese there was no way the request for an approval would be granted. The hall was packed and I could tell afterward the people felt very bad for the position my superiors had put me in. They were angrier than ever with the bishop, thinking even less of him for putting me in the position he did, thinking he was either cowardly or vicious.

That day and that night was critical for me. When I went home, my blood pressure was 220 over 150. My blood pressure medicine would not bring it down. I probably should have gone to the hospital, but I was too stressed out, and just wanted to go to bed. The next day was the CROP walk for starving people and I figured the eight mile walk would bring down my pressure. I needed to be part of that project to lead the people. And, when the walk was over, even though I had blisters on my feet, my pressure had dropped to an almost reasonable level, 155 over 127. When I got back to the rectory, I was tired, so I just collapsed on the bed and fell sound asleep, I don't know how long I slept. I had not slept well the night before, so that rest was needed. All that I have just described about this housing issue took place over a 19-month period, and I telescoped it all together in these few pages so it would make more sense. The mess dogged my whole time in the parish. There was not a day when it was not weighing heavily on my mind, and on the people's minds as well. My doctor was especially concerned because of the effect it was having on my health.

The next morning, when I went over to church for morning Mass, I thanked God for air conditioning. The previous summer, we had broken through the brick walls in four corners of the church and instilled 10,000 BTU units which cooled off the church nicely. So, offering Mass each morning was pleasant.

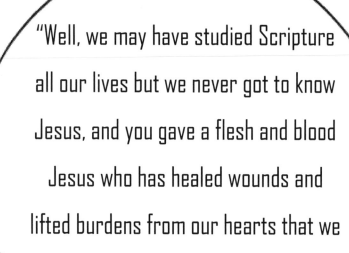

"Well, we may have studied Scripture all our lives but we never got to know Jesus, and you gave a flesh and blood Jesus who has healed wounds and lifted burdens from our hearts that we had carried all our life."

Chapter Fifteen

I thought that going to a sleepy little village down along the Hudson would be a quiet and serene oasis from the whirlwind in Amsterdam. But, it was not to be. The haunting housing issue I had to put into a mental compartment so I could deal with other pressing problems. It was a good thing I didn't have psychological problems as the bishop had told me, or what I was going through there would have pushed me over the edge.

As cold weather approached which necessitated turning on the heat in the rectory and the church and school, I noticed that no matter how high we turned up the thermostat in the church, it was always cold. I asked some older parishioners what they thought the reason might be, and why it was never dealt with before. No one seemed to know. One day, with a pair of binoculars, I looked closely at the ceiling between the rafters and saw that there was bare wood, which meant that there was no insulation. The wood was only three quarters of an inch thick. When the heat was turned on it went up to the ceiling and right out through the roof, and never had a chance to work its way back down to the pew level. So, it was always cold, especially in the bitterly cold days in deep winter.

What to do seemed impossible to resolve. The parish income was meager. There were a lot of poor people in the parish, though the majority were working people with relatively good jobs. Some had their own businesses. There were also many professional people.

Again, for some reason they were not in the habit of giving generous donations to the church, and I was never any good at raising money. I always felt that if the priest was doing his job, the people would respond accordingly, without being asked. Time would tell.

While trying to figure out what to do about the church roof, there was another very pressing problem. Many of the children in the parish were going to the Protestant churches for their religious instructions, and I needed to bring those little sheep back home. I was not at all impressed with our parish's religious instruction program, and knew something had to be done. A crisis was precipitated at the same time as the housing crisis arose. One night, the religious education director called the rectory to tell me that there was a large group of parishioners in the hall, demanding to talk to me. I had no idea what this was all about. I found out later that the other priest was so disappointed that he was not made pastor, he was determined to drive me out of the parish, so he spread the rumor that I was a radical liberal and if the people allowed me to remain as pastor, I would destroy the parish.

When I went over to the school hall, it was like walking into a hornet's nest. "What is this we hear that you are not going to let our children make their First Communion and Confirmation?"

I was very honest with them and told them that I had no idea where they could have heard such a thing. I explained to them how important First Communion and Confirmation were, and that I did

198

have a plan to improve the programs so the children would be better prepared. I told them that, "ever since I started working in parishes, I watched to see what happened to the children who made their First Communion. After a month or so they stopped receiving and many stopped going to Mass, and come back only when it was time for their Confirmation years later. I was appalled. When I made my own First Communion as a child I used to get up and go to Mass every morning so I could be close to Jesus, and I continued that through my whole life. It troubled me deeply that children seem to have no understanding of what the Eucharist really is, and that is because we are not teaching them in the right way. So, I am not denying children their First Communion, but I am going to start a program to make sure that the whole attitude towards Communion can be changed. This can be done only if the whole family is part of the preparation for this beautiful Sacrament. And I intend also to be part of the program. I intend to hold classes for the parents for a five-week period, once a week, and teach the basic beliefs about what it means to be Christian and the theology of the Eucharist. Then I expect the parents to teach their own children about their faith and what Communion should mean to them. This is critical because so many parents never talk to their children about these things and when they have to learn it from a stranger, and, like a skin graft from a stranger; it never takes. So, if the parents are really concerned about Communion meaning something to the children they should be thrilled to be part of the preparation. Then, as each child is prepared, the parents will bring the child to the rectory, where I will question him or her, and in a very informal way, ask the child if he or she has done anything to offend God, or someone in their family, or anyone else. It will be very unthreatening and relaxed so they will have a good experience for their first confession, then I will give them their penance and absolution. In the past where I have done this, the children always enjoyed this part of their preparation. And I intend also to do something similar with preparation for Confirmation, once I get your children back from the Protestant churches."

At the end of the evening, I was drained but the people seemed pleased and realized they had been led astray by what they had been told. They were very pleasant towards me as the meeting broke up. Only a few parents balked at having to teach their kids, and I told them that they should be proud to prepare their children for Communion rather than have a stranger teach them.

It turned out well. The individual kids made their First Communion, just like the ones in Our Lady of Mount Carmel, together with their parents. When all the children had done it this way, we then had them all come together on a set Sunday and had them all receive Communion together, and had a party afterwards.

With that big concern over, I had to do something about insulating the church roof. I talked to a few men and asked for suggestions. I told them there was no way we could afford to have a contractor do the job. I checked our financial situation and knew we could afford to buy the materials, but could not afford to hire a company to do the work. Tommy O'Neill and a few others offered to do the work. Finally, 10 or 12 others joined in and we had a good work crew. The liveliest of the bunch was Jimmy Frangella, who was in his late seventies. Frank Hogan, another enthusiastic volunteer, was an engineer working at Atlantic Cement and could borrow the scaffolding from the company and have it delivered to the church. The men put all the sections together. Once the inch-thick Styrofoam sheets were delivered, the men came to the church after work each night, and on Saturdays. A crew climbed up on top of the scaffolding some thirty feet high at the peak, and put the insulation between the rafters, while another crew below cut the pieces so they would fit perfectly into place. It took them almost two weeks to do the whole job, then we were told we had to cover the Styrofoam with sheetrock, which was a big disappointment, but we had the sheetrock delivered. The men cut that too, and sent it up to the platform above and that was put into place. We used small pieces of wood, one inch by three inches by half inch and nailed them to the rafters at strategic places to secure the sheetrock. Then another crew followed them and painted the sheetrock the same color as the rafters and previous ceiling between the rafters. When it was finished, it looked no different than before. The whole job was done for not much more than -a $1,000 dollar. It would have cost us at least $15,000 if we had a company do it. My job was to keep them in pizza and drinks for the whole time. I was their Gunga Din. We all felt so good when it was finished. It did not take long before we felt the effect in the church.

As soon as the cold weather came, it was a joy to turn on the furnace. Within a few minutes the church started to warm. It worked and everyone felt so proud that they had done it all themselves.

The summers, however, were hot and it was most oppressive when there were weddings, and everyone was dressed so elegantly. Also, extremely hot weather is more dangerous to old people than cold. I knew we had to have air conditioning. The problem is that engineers calculated what is needed by the number of cubic feet. I felt we didn't need to cool the ceiling, just about eight feet up from the floor. So, on my own, I had a couple of the men puncture holes through the walls of the church and installed 20,000 BTU air conditioners in the four corners of the church. I knew the four units would work because they worked in Amsterdam. Now with the newly insulated roof, the air conditioners worked perfectly. So, when we had daily Mass, and weekend Masses, and weddings on hot afternoons the church was delightfully cool. When winter came that year, for the first time, the church was toasty warm and the oil usage dropped dramatically.

Before the end of my first year at Saint Patrick's, which was in the spring of 1979 we had our Confirmation. A lot had to be done before we could prepare for that. Getting the parents to bring their children back to the parish was a problem. It necessitated a change in the religion program in the parish. I had to get a director who had the allegiance of all the parents, and even though she did not have her certification from the diocese, she was the only one capable of getting all the children back into the parish for their religion classes. Pat O'Neil was her name. She was Lebanese, married to Tommy O'Neill, who was one of the most active volunteers on the church insulation job, and whose family was well respected in the parish. Pat had an excellent background in her religion and kept up in her theological studies. Most importantly, she had been a teacher in the local public school system and had taught practically every parent in the parish. They all loved her and respected her. However, the nun who was the diocesan director at the chancery harassed me then, for years afterwards, for not having a certified parish director. She had no idea the mess the parish was in, and I could afford neither the time nor the money to go through the process of finding a stranger to come into the parish to teach our children. It could have been disastrous if we had hired the wrong person.

As it turned out, in no time at all, the parents brought all the children back into the parish and gladly sent them to their dear friend's religion program. When it came time for their Confirmation the following spring, there were so many children being confirmed, the bishop said he could not do them all one day, but would come back the following week and confirm the other half of the group. It worked out beautifully. By spring time, we also had two choirs in the parish, a traditional choir for the first Confirmation group, and a folk choir for the second Confirmation group. Our music director, Ted Smith, was perfect for the parish. He was a music teacher at the local high school, and I was fortunate in talking him into taking on the music program in the parish. He was wonderful with the choirs, and had a good sense of liturgical music. He played the organ, directed the choir, and trained a good quality folk choir. The previous organist was well on in age and, I did not have the heart to fire her. I talked to her one day, and asked her if it was too demanding of her to keep working. "If you were my mother, Kitty, I would not let you work, but I don't want to make decisions for you, but I am going to make you an offer, if you want to accept it."

"What is that, Father?"

"I know you don't have a pension, so if you choose to take a rest and retire, I will still pay you your salary. That will be your pension for your faithful work for the parish all these years."

She had tears in your eyes. "I think I will take your offer, Father. I would have retired long ago if I had a pension. And, Father Joe, I have to tell you. You have the nicest way of firing somebody. Thank you, and know that I love you, and I always will."

"I know, and I love you, too, Kitty."

When the bishop came back the second week, and found such a happy group of people just like the previous week, he was impressed. In the rectory, afterwards, when he was socializing with the parish trustees and other key parishioners, he told Doctor Whalen and Jimmy Frangella what a fine job they did in turning the parish around from the horrible state it had been in. He told them he thought it would take at least three years to get things back on track. Doctor Whalen laughed and said, "We didn't do thing, bishop, Father Girzone did it all by himself. He's the one you should thank." Doctor Whalen told me that afterwards, and I was happy to find out that the bishop was pleased, but not so happy to find out that he also knew what a mess the parish was in before he assigned me there. Then, I realized for the first time that there probably were not 13 other priests who wanted the parish, as the bishop had told me. There were probably 13 who turned it down.

During all this time, I was most fortunate to have the loyalty of the trustees, who by this time had become dear friends, and also the loyalty of the parish lawyer, John Biscone and his wife Mary. John assured me that whatever decisions I had to make he would support me. His whole family had also become friends. Dennis Whalen, like his father, had married a beautiful Italian girl, and I had the joy of baptizing their children. The members of the parish council were also supportive, and for the remainder of my time there we were all able to accomplish miracles in the parish with God's help.

Since the very beginning of my stay there one of my greatest comforts was a wonderful little family, who had dropped off a pumpkin for me on the rectory porch the very first week I arrived. Judy Van Alstine had three of the most beautiful adopted children, Jennifer, Kristin and Paula, whom I loved as if they were my own. We still keep in touch though they now live so far away in New

Hampshire. The five of us had such wonderful times together; they brought sunshine into my life during those very difficult times.

Once the Confirmation was over, I knew I had to do something to get back home a lot of the parishioners who had fallen away from the parish. I met so many of them as I walked around the parish. Also, family members used to tell which members of their families I should talk to as they had not been in church for years. That was fun, because I knew many of them already and they told me they were wondering how long it would take before I started hauling them all back to Mass. One of the problems, however, was that they had a hard time going to confession since they were so upset about things that had happened in the parish and run-ins they had had with the bishop and previous priests. I knew the only way I could get them back to Communion was if I had general confession, where they would not have to make a detailed admission face to face of all that they had done.

I had the same problem at Mount Carmel, and was able to get the majority of the people back to church that way, before I left the parish. I felt uneasy doing it, but it was the only solution. I felt more comfortable with it after the bishop invited Father Walsh, a theologian from Washington, to speak to all the priests in the diocese about the Sacrament of Reconciliation and General Confession. During that talk, I told the speaker how I did it my parish in Amsterdam, by preparing the people beforehand and then at the penance service spelling out a long list of ways we could offend God or our neighbor, and telling the people to say quietly to God that they were sorry, if they recognized a sin they had committed. I would then give them absolution. The speaker confirmed that that was a good way to do it. Behind me at the time were two Franciscan priests from Siena College. One was the president. I could hear the other priest talking about me, saying that I sounded nervous. The president said, "Don't be fooled. He's got one of the sharpest minds in the diocese, and every word is carefully weighed. He's just letting the bishop know what he's doing, knowing the speaker will approve of it in front of the whole diocese."

I was surprised the president of Siena even knew me. I later approached the bishop to tell him that I hoped I did not put him on the spot. He said no, and that he agreed that that's the way it should be done. And I am sure that that was the reason he invited that priest to speak to us all.

So, I felt comfortable doing the same thing down in Ravena, knowing that the bishop agreed with what I had done in Amsterdam, and knowing how important it was in drawing the wandering sheep back into the flock. I scheduled a general confession and absolution, and as in Amsterdam, the church was filled to overflow, some standing outside the church. Many wandering sheep returned home that night.

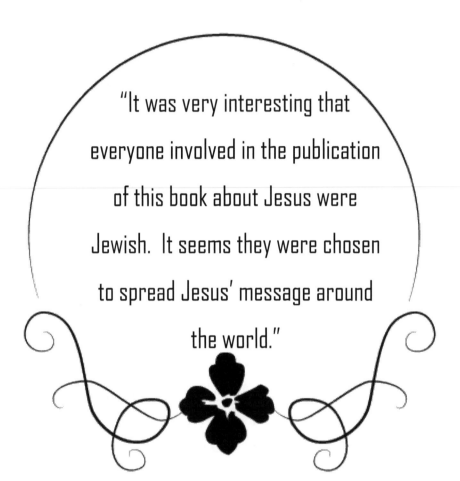

"It was very interesting that everyone involved in the publication of this book about Jesus were Jewish. It seems they were chosen to spread Jesus' message around the world."

Chapter Sixteen

If I seem to ramble, it is because so many things happened in my two years in Ravena that were related to things that happened at different times, it is hard not to jump around to tie together loose ends, and show how decisions eventually turned out. Not long after I got settled in the parish, I got a phone call from the Commissioner of the Office on Aging for Albany County. He told me he learned that I was the new pastor in Ravena, which was in Albany County, and said he had been following on television and the news on what I had done in Schenectady and Amsterdam, and said he would like to work with me in Albany County. He was very upfront in a humorous way, told me he knew I could be trouble to the politicians when things were not going the way they should. "So, I just wanted to let you know, I will help you in whatever way I can?" He was a friendly fellow and was serious about the situation of the elderly in that far end of the county.

I said, "As a matter of fact there is. There are a lot of people living out in Coeymans Hollow who are elderly and isolated, and living in life threatening conditions, and we can help them if we have help from the county. Also, we need a congregate meals program here in the village and "Meals on Wheels" program for the town which is extends out over eight miles. Our parish school is closed so we can offer the kitchen and cafeteria in lieu of local share of funding, if you want to use it. And we will help in whatever way we can to provide help for the elderly population."

The commissioner was delighted. He said he would give us funding to renovate the kitchen and ready the cafeteria for congregate meals. The county would also pay the heat bill for the building. He told us we needed to set up a corporation to run the operation, and appoint officers, and open a bank account for the monies the county would send for the operation. We also had to have our own local share of funding to receive state and federal funding for various programs. After that conversation with the commissioner, it took only a month or two before we were up and running. It took us a while longer to buy a van to drive the seniors to various events in Albany and to go shopping. We got the specially equipped van to deliver hot meals to the elderly throughout the vast township. We also set up a bank account, and the board of directors decided to have bingo to raise money for the project. We took in over five hundred dollars each week. At the time New York State Gas and Electric was having trouble with people complaining about the dangers of nuclear power, so their stock dropped to just a few dollars a share. However, their dividend stayed the same, and at the price of the stock, the dividend was still 14%. We put all the money we could into NYSG&E stock. Before long we had well over 1000 shares, and it rose to many more gradually. As the price went up the value of our stock skyrocketed, but we were still getting 14% on the original amount we invested.

Now, since so many senior citizens were coming to the parish hall for their meals we thought we should fix up the grounds in front of the building which was right on the main street through the village. I got a crew together and an excellent mason, and we dug a trench all around the ground in front of the building. The space was about 30'x30.' That was my job. I was good at digging the trench. Electric wires were then put in the ground for electric outlets, and for lights later. We then had a load of concrete delivered, and poured into the ditch. In two days, the men started building the brick wall, with bricks donated by the brickyard company just outside the village. In a couple of weeks, the wall was finished and antique lamps were put in place on those sections of the wall that were built like little columns in strategic places along the wall and in the corners. We then had picnic tables made and put colored umbrellas in each table. We now had our courtyard and our picnic tables and in another week, we had our first ice cream social. We were open every night, and the people who came to Mass in the morning gathered in the patio for coffee and donuts afterwards in nice weather. On Sunday after Mass, people gathered there to socialize before going home. In no time, that little space brought the whole village together. People came from all over the village, changing the whole community atmosphere. Parish life had come alive and so many good things were happening. The old folks were being taken care of, the children found church a happy experience, especially the little kids who looked forward to standing around the altar with me from the offertory. They loved to do that. I know it

211

was not good liturgical practice, but I knew Jesus would do it, and it inspired the little ones to pester their fathers to take them to church so they could go up on the altar with the priest. The children were beginning to like priests again and liked going to church; not very common anymore.

While I was at Saint Patrick's I was asked by the New York State Division for Youth if I would consider being on their Independent Review Board which was an oversight group that monitored conditions in the almost 50 youth prisons in the state. The director told me they needed someone with common sense on the board and asked if I would seriously consider it. It would entail going with the other members to a different prison every other month, and observe and assess conditions in each of them and then make reports. I eventually accepted, as I thought it would take me away from the stressful problems in the parish for a day every other month, which it did. The drive to each of these sites was peaceful and healing, and I learned a lot about how young children are treated in these youth prisons. Only a few places in the state seemed to have a wholesome policy and they were the places operated by the Christian Brothers. One was LaSalle in Albany, and the other was Lincoln Hall in lower New York State, just above Yonkers. They had good discipline, good healthy meals, good sports programs, and most importantly a very well-run school where the children attended classes every day. Education was lacking in most state schools, where often the children were just warehoused. The recompense for our work was nominal, just mileage money and a small token check for our service.

At the same time, I was still on another board, for Niagara Mohawk Power Corporation. I had been on that since I was at Mount Carmel, and after I got the reputation for investigating the death of the Bakers in Schenectady after their power was turned off in the middle of winter. That advisory board was important because it gave us direct input to the top officials at the power company and all of us on the board were very vocal, and said just what we felt about issues. Some were people-oriented and some had high-up friends in the company. The process for ending electrical service for a delinquent customer was made more humane, and people were given much more consideration than before. Also, payment plans were adapted to people's ability to pay. One significant issue concerned problems associated with nuclear power generation. One issue was cost overruns. The power company was always blamed for cost overruns which the consumer would eventually have to pay for. We insisted on an investigation on why there were such high cost overruns, and by the end of the investigation, it became clear that the State Public Service Commission had people on their board who were opposed to nuclear power and looked for any excuse to stop construction. At our last meeting on the subject, which was held at the Public Service Commission's offices in Albany, I asked for information that the PSC officials were unwilling to provide. My question was, "How much of the cost of the overruns was due to the Public Service Commission's orders for work stoppage. After I had made myself totally obnoxious, they finally gave us the information. Close to 70% of the cost overruns were due, not to Niagara Mohawk's faulty estimates, but to the Public Service Commission's frequent ordered shut-downs.

The other problem with nuclear power generation was disposal of heavily toxic waste. We invited a very liberal spokesman for the scientific groups opposed to nuclear power to come and speak to our board. He arrived an hour late, casually dressed in sport clothes and sneakers, and began telling us all about the negative issues involving nuclear energy, things we had already heard many times over. I asked him what the greatest problem was with nuclear power generation, and he said, "Waste disposal." I then asked him, "Is there any way that that problem could be solved?" His answer was, "Well, yes, if you really want go that route." "You didn't answer the question. Is there any way to solve that problem?" "Well, if you insist on it, there is. The French have solved it, but I am not here to promote nuclear power." "But, would you please be gracious enough to tell us how the French scientists solved that problem?" He finally gave us the information. "They vitrify it and make it into glass cakes, then put it into deep underground mines where it can never be of any harm to anyone, and cannot leach out into underground water supplies." "Thank you."

After that I was asked to make the committee's report on the issue of nuclear power generation for our group. That was about my only contribution in the whole six or seven years I was on the board.

Some of the others were much more involved and had a day to day understanding of issues of much greater concern to the ordinary consumers, and made much more worthwhile contributions than I did. Since it was a voluntary board, the compensation was limited to reimbursement for mileage to and from the meetings.

Those two board meetings were not a distraction from parish work; as most of my time driving to and from the meetings was taken up analyzing situations in the parish, and trying to understand what was the best way to provide a warm experience for the people's involvement with the parish. Two men in the parish were very close friends, Mr. Clean, as the people called one fellow who was of the same build as Mr. Clean on television, and his friend, Allie Pape. They used to stop up to the rectory every few days just to chat. It was so nice of them and I appreciated their friendship. It helped to lift my spirits to know they felt I was their friend, because it was a very difficult time for me. They both came from important families in the parish. Allie was a cousin of Gilda Libertucci, my secretary at Mount Carmel, my previous parish.

There were other Libertuccis in Saint Patrick's. One was a very good ceramic artist. When I discovered that, I got an idea how I could liven up the atmosphere in the church. I decided I would make two mosaics, to fit on each of the two sides of the sanctuary. On the right side, I planned a place for the tabernacle containing the Blessed Sacrament. The tabernacle would be set in front of a 4'

8' red mosaic, with bright rays coming from above, and letters in gold "Whoever eats this Bread will live forever."

Vi. Libertucci made all the tiles for me. With special hand cutters, I broke the tiles into tiny mosaic chips, and glued them in place over the drawing I did on the ¾" plywood. In all there were about 10,000 little pieces in place when I finished. It took me months, usually after most of the village was asleep. It was a quiet, peaceful time for me, and good therapy for my stress. The other mosaic was for the wall on the left and was for the bible. I had bought a copy of the scriptures with a beautiful gold plated sterling silver hinged cover, with engravings on it. It was very fitting to show the importance of scripture in our liturgy. Again, Mrs. Libertucci made these gorgeous sky blue tiles and the gold tiles I needed for the lettering, "Behold, the inspired word of God." That mosaic also had about 10,000 chips in it when I finished. The gold covered book of the scriptures was set in place in front of that mosaic and when we used it for liturgy, the altar servers or the priest would reverently remove it from its place and bring it to the lectern for the lector. I was so happy that I could put the scriptures in a nice setting. For a good while after I finished that project my hands pained from straining the muscles for such long periods of time, but in time they healed.

Chapter Seventeen

During my time in Ravena, I kept in touch with my Korean friends in Canada. I finally received labor certification for them, and approval for them to enter the country and obtain their green card. Now that I was in another parish, I had a seemingly insurmountable problem. The labor certification specified that they would be working in Our Lady of Mount Carmel parish in Amsterdam, New York. I talked to the pastor of my previous parish, told him the situation and asked if we could work out a solution to the problem. After a few days when I called him back, and asked if there was anything he could do to help, he said he talked to the bishop's office and the answer was "No." Very few things really get me angry, but I was furious at the attitude of some people, as I would always try to bend as much as I possibly could to help somebody in need. I could never understand this kind of attitude in fellow priests, but I believed the pastor when he said the bishop's office told him not to help me with the problem.

The only alternative was to ask God to help. The situation was totally impossible, and I knew I could never go through that horrible process with immigration again. Time would not allow it. I prayed hard, and I knew God would help, as he always did, even though the situation seemed impossible.

At about the same time as this situation came to a critical point, I got a telephone call from some dear friends from the old parish in

Scotia. The call was from Rose Ferro. She and her husband and their family were wonderful friends. Her husband, Dominick, though everyone called him, "Skinny." "Skinny" Ferro, was a dear friend. His wife asked if I could please visit Dom in the hospital, as he was asking for me. I drove up to the hospital which was about twenty-five miles away. When I went into my friend's room, I could see he was very weak. We always had a rather interesting relationship. He was very conservative in his approach not only to religion but to everything else, especially politics. He was one of those friends of mine whose salvation was that they married their guardian angel. Dom was a top union official at the main General Electric plant in Schenectady. He was also a staunch Republican and a longtime member of the Sons of Italy, another very conservative organization. We seemed to be at the very opposite ends of everything we talked about, except our concern for people. He had the kindest heart for anybody who was hurting. I always told him that even though he was a Republican in everything else, he had a Democratic heart when it came to helping people in need. That always got me a real dirty look and a grunt. But, in spite of all our differences, we deeply loved each other.

When I entered his room, and went over to the bed, I kissed him on his forehead, and said, "Skinny, what the hell are you doing here? I thought you were too damned ornery to get sick."

"Father, I'm dying."

I felt like I got a punch in the stomach. I could always take a lot, but that was too much. It was hard to lose such a friend.

"I wanted you to come here so I could ask you if you would say my funeral Mass."

"Skinny, I would love to do your funeral."

"Darn you, you don't have to be so happy about it."

"I'm not really, Skinny, it's just that it's such a shock, I can't take it seriously."

"Well, it is serious. I don't have but a few days."

"Skinny, I am so sorry. Tell me what happened."

He told me the whole story about his illness, and it was a very sad time.

"Well, I am sure you are ready. Anything we should talk about?"

"No, Father, I'm at peace. We can't live forever. My job's done."

"If it has to be, it has to be. Your kindness to hurting people will assure you of a special jet to heaven. I will try to give you the best send off a man could have. Even though you have such a crusty exterior, I must admit, you do have the heart of a saint, and I know when God takes you home, there won't be any stopping off places. You'll be going right straight home."

After talking to him about heaven and praying with him, he thanked me for coming and said, "You're a good priest, Father, and I want to thank you for being willing to do my funeral. We then hugged each other with the Italian kiss, and said goodbye. And I left. I am sure we both had heavy hearts. It was a long way back to Ravena.

Skinny died a few days later. We thought the funeral would be in two or three days, but his wife, Rose, called to say the funeral had to be postponed because their son, Benedict, could not get away from his work for another couple of days.

I asked her, "What does Benny do."

"He's the director of immigration for New York State, and he is tied up with a difficult problem. Besides there will be federal officials coming from Washington and other places for the funeral, so we have to plan for their arrival."

I could not believe what Rose was telling me. Who says that God is not aware of what's going on in our lives? I am convinced he is an intimate partner with each of us if we only allow him. What a chance to deliver a critical message to the top immigration officials in the country! And my dear friend Skinny's son is the director of immigration for the whole state, and can make decisions without going to anyone else. How did Skinny know I needed that kind of help? Who says saints can't help?

Benny came a day or two later, and we made arrangements for the wake and the Mass. I said nothing about my Korean friends until after the funeral when I went with the family for the reception planned for all the visitors.

For the Mass the church was packed, not just with family friends and GE officials and workers, but immigration officials from Washington and from all across the state, and local politicians, and members of the Sons of Italy, and local parishioners. I tried to make the Mass a good experience for the family, who were always such gracious people as well as dear friends. When it came time to read the Gospel, and give the sermon, I read the part of the Gospel where Jesus talks about the last judgment, "Come, blessed of my Father, into the kingdom prepared for you from the beginning of time. When I was hungry, you gave me food; when I was thirsty, you gave me drink; when I was naked, you clothed me; when I was ill, you cared for me; when I was in prison, you visited me, when I was a stranger you welcomed me.' And they will ask, 'When Lord did we see you hungry or thirsty or naked, or ill, or in prison, or a stranger and care for you?' And the Lord will answer, 'As long as you did it to the least of my brothers and sisters, you did it to me."

"This morning we pay tribute to our dear friend Dominick. I still remember the first day I saw him when I came to the parish. I was offering the eight o'clock Mass, and Dom walked into the back of the church and sat down over to the left there in the back pew. I was impressed. That little gesture of shyness and humility expressed his whole life. He never made a big splash. He was a Republican, very conservative in so many things, except in union business, then he was more like a radical Democrat. But what impressed me most about his life was his deep concern for troubled people. He was always there to help a person who was going through genuinely difficult times and needed help. It was that sensitivity to hurting people that brought the two of us close, while we disagreed on just about everything else. But, we loved each other deeply. I have no doubt that Dominick is now a saint, even though his family may have other thoughts about that.

In matters of his faith, Dominick was always loyal. He had a simple, almost childlike faith, which is so beautiful in a person today. It served him well in the difficult atmosphere of changing fashions in religion these days. For a priest, the climate today is a challenge in many ways, particularly in areas that touch on both religion and politics. I have had people say to me quite often, 'You priests should stay out of politics. You're supposed to preach religion.' The moral aspects of politics are very much the sphere of a priest's concern, because it affects the lives of the people. One of the areas that is very sensitive is immigration. To so many people around the world, America is heaven to them, and they try in every way to enter our American paradise. It is a most difficult issue for all of us and an area where we have to be very careful how we treat people trying so desperately to flee destitution and other life-threatening situations in their own countries. Often it may be only imminent starvation, but that too can be life threatening. To find a safe haven where they can find work and save their families, does not make them criminals, but refugees from starvation. And all of us should remember that one day we will be refugees from our own country, not to another country on this earth, but to a kingdom where we will be applying for citizenship, the kingdom of heaven. All of us, even the best of us, in the eyes of that King, are violators of his laws all during our lives, which he will be willing to overlook, as he has promised, but only on one condition, that we treat others, the hungry, the thirsty, the naked, the ill, the imprisoned, and yes, the starving refugees, with compassion. He made it very clear, that when we apply for citizenship in his kingdom, he will judge us in the same way we have judged others.

I have no doubt that our dear friend Dom will have no trouble in arriving there. His own kindness and compassion will assure him of a merciful judgment, and one day we all hope that our own judgment, when that time comes, will also be merciful."

It was a difficult homily to give, but it was a statement that was necessary under the circumstances. Fortunately, in meeting so many of the people afterwards, no one seemed to be offended, and I even got some positive comments, especially from immigration officials who felt they had made a retreat.

What did happen which was very positive, was that I had a chance to talk to Dominick's son afterwards, and he said if I ever needed any help, he would be happy to help in whatever way he could. "Benny, you don't know how much that means to me. In fact, I have a problem right now, and hopefully you might be able to help, if you can." I then proceeded to tell him about my friends, the Lim family. After telling him the whole story, he said that he would work something out so the family could come back from Canada. In a few days, the whole matter was cleared up, and a short time later the Lims were living down near Ravena, and began helping Korean people in the wider area by teaching their children their religion. After doing a fine job, they later moved to Florida, and shortly later became American citizens and Mr. Lim did very well in his business there, so when he died only a few years later, his family was assured of, at least, a dignified livelihood, and their treasured American citizenship.

Chapter Eighteen

Parish life seemed never to get dull or boring. For some reason or other, problems always sprang up and dropped in my lap. I often wondered if the same things happened in other priests' lives. I hardly ever had a day when something did not occur which demanded some kind of creative solution. Creating solutions was what was difficult, but then, I suppose that is the way we grow. For a long time, I was realizing that all the unusual happenings were not haphazard, but part of a training process for the future, as my knowledge of Jesus was deepening. So, all the disjointed happenings in my life remained just that, disjointed events. I never knew what was going to happen each day when I started the day. I never had to go out and look for something to do. Things just happened, all different and seemingly none of them connected.

One day a young man, in his early twenties came to visit me. He was from a prominent family in the parish. He shared with me an extremely serious problem that frightened me, because as he described it to me, I knew that if I helped him, I could get into serious trouble. He was in the Marines. He had been stationed at Twenty-Nine Palms, in southern California. He had been injured one day when a cannon blast went off near him and punctured his ear drum, causing intense pain as it got infected. He told me that when he asked to go to the doctor he was refused permission. His superior did not believe he really had a problem, and thought he was faking. This went on for a long time. "As I was hurting more and more, I started getting angry, and was developing a dangerous attitude which frightened me. I was so upset one day, when I was driving a tank, I could see headquarters in front of me and had the strongest urge to drive the tank right through headquarters. I knew then I was cracking up, and I got scared. I asked if I could at least talk to the commanding general. I was denied that permission three times."

"Did you ever talk with the chaplain?" I asked him.

"No, Father, I had reason to feel he was on the side of the officers, and I was afraid to share anything with him."

"So, now that you are home on leave, what are your plans?"

"Father, I don't want to go back. I am afraid I am going to do something terrible. I need help bad. I really think I am cracking up."

"Did you get your ear problem taken care of?"

"Recently I did, and it seems to be healing."

In watching the young man's body movements and changing facial expressions, I could tell he was very disturbed emotionally, which did not seem to be part of his normal personality. I knew the family well. Not being a psychiatrist, there was nothing I could do to help him with his emotional or mental problems. I was worried, however, as he did not have much of his leave left before he had to return to base. So, I told him to go to his family lawyer, and make a complete statement of what had happened at the base, and "make sure you are honest and tell every detail as accurately as you possibly can. This affidavit can be used as a court document if it is ever needed, but make sure you are truthful. That is absolutely critical. Then tell your lawyer to hold the affidavits until the right time. Also, I think you should go to the Veterans hospital, not to a private psychiatrist, or any other hospital. At the Veterans Hospital, there are military doctors who will be up to date on proper military protocol. You may need that kind of support."

He went to his lawyer and went to the Veterans Hospital in Albany. The doctor said he needed help immediately and kept him in the hospital long past the time for him to return to base. Around Christmas time, the doctor let him spend time at home, when he came to see me and bring me up to date. He said the doctor would still not release him, but just allowed him to have a home visit. The captain at the base called and demanded that he return to base immediately, and said that if he didn't come they would have to take further action to bring him back. At that time, the young man was allowed by the doctor to be an outpatient at the hospital. Now he was really scared that the MPs would come and arrest him, and put him in the brig, and that he would then surely "go nuts." I told him not to worry about that and if that time ever came he could stay in the rectory and we would do what we had to do. If they try to take you from the rectory, we will have a big issue to deal with, but we can deal with that if we have to. I wrote to the bishop and told him the situation, and that I might have to keep the boy in the

227

rectory, and that there might be a serious problem if the MPs came and to arrest him. This was something the bishop should know before it happens, as there was a very serious possibility that there could be a confrontation with the government. I was hoping I would get a return letter, or at least a phone call, with some suggestion, or different way of handling the problem, or an expression of support, but it didn't come.

At that point I was really nervous. I decided to call my friend Sam Stratton, who, as chairman of the House Armed Services Committee, and whose home was Amsterdam, had always been such a help in situations in the past involving military issues. He did do a thorough check with officials at the base and they convinced him that the boy was wrong, so Sam told me that he was sorry that he was unable to help.

We got through the Christmas holidays, and for a while things were quiet, so I went on a spiritual retreat for a few days. During the retreat, the Marine chaplain called, and my secretary gave him my number at the retreat house. He tried to impress on me that it was very important that I send the young man back to camp. He told me that the captain was quite insistent that I let the fellow return to base, and was determined to do what had to be done to get the young man back to the base.

I then lost my cool. "Now I know why the boy never went to see you when he was having problems. He told me he could not trust you. I can see why; you have sold your soul to the military and your interest is in your own position as an officer rather than protecting and helping the young fellows under your care."

I then told him that there was no way that I would let the boy go back there.

The priest said nothing, then after a pause, said very humbly, "Father, please pray for me." I felt bad that I had hurt him so deeply. I should have been more understanding of his difficult position, but I was not in a very understanding frame of mine. And his phone call ruined my retreat, which I cut short to return to Ravena to make sure nothing would be done while I was away.

As soon as I returned from the retreat, I called the boy to the rectory and told him that this was the time to tell his lawyer to send the affidavits to the Commanding General at the base. They were sent out by certified mail that day. It was not long before we heard from the general's office. The general had a thorough investigation into all the facts of the case, and was furious, especially because the young man was denied permission to talk to his commanding general, which permission apparently should never be denied to a person in the service. The lawyer at the base was sent back to law school for more training. The boy's sergeant was demoted for refusing to allow the young man medical attention. The captain was severely censured, and the young man was told to come back to base with the assurance that his case would be handled fairly. That we could go along with, since it was clear the general seemed like a decent human being who could be trusted. The boy went back and a short time later was given a medical discharge.

Even though there were so many difficult problems in the parish, there were happy times, and times when good things happened. One happening in the parish that was a fun project and a healthy distraction from the stressful issues. That was a project that sort of fell into our laps. It was with the local television company. They had an unused channel. I thought if we could get the use of that channel it could be of valuable benefit to the parish, and the whole neighborhood. It was a community access channel. I called the company and they said they would be happy if we could put it to good use. They agreed to let us use it and sent their technicians up to install the necessary connection equipment on the utility pole outside the rectory and connect it to an outlet in the rectory. That gave us our own television studio, to be used in any way that was of benefit to the parish and the community. We connected it also with the church, and started having a televised Mass on Sundays for the shut-ins in the neighborhood. It could also be used for special celebrations in the church, for Confirmations and First Communions, and any concerts that might be held in the church. I also bought a batch of beautiful movies from the Paulist Publications and showed them over the channel. This provided good inspirational movies for the parish, and for the whole neighborhood. They were not Catholic movies, but movies about God and faith, and movies that could be used to inspire children. These public access channels were available all through the 13 counties of the diocese. It was, I thought, something the people of the whole 13 counties could benefit from if the diocese could get hold of them before someone else did. What I wanted to eventually do was put the whole religious education program on the television, and with the cable company extending their lines out into Coeymans Hollow, the outer part of the parish, some eight miles distant, it would be possible then to speak to the whole parish, among other things, and also have a few excellent religious education teachers conduct exciting classes for the young people. We could also have parent involvement in two way conversations, during call-ins. Getting qualified teachers for religion was always difficult, and diocesan certification did not certify that they were good at their work, but that they took the courses required. I wanted excellent teachers. That was one of the reasons I myself took part in that program in parishes where I was stationed, even though I was not certified, so that I could have input in what the children and high school confirmation age students were learning.

Being far from the city brought people together because they needed each other. That was one reason the television cable was such a help. Another nice thing about being in a small village was the comradeship among clergy who could help each other when needed. The local ministers at times had a difficult time getting a replacement in an emergency. Joe Ingraham, the Methodist pastor and I remained good friends the whole time I was in Ravena, and we would occasionally exchange pulpits for various events. One time, his wife Mary's parents were in a horrible automobile accident way out in Seattle, Washington. They had to leave and be with her folks, so Joe called and asked if I could take his Sunday services at the Methodist church. I told him I would be glad to. So, when Sunday came, I offered my scheduled Masses in the parish, and conducted the Sunday service at the Methodist church. The people were appreciative, and very grateful. Mary and Joe were happy and felt relieved I could cover for them, and I felt good about being able to help my friend in a time of need.

However, someone in my own parish must have called the chancery, complaining that I was doing Sunday services in a Protestant church. Naturally, I got a call from the chancellor. "Is it true you did the services in a Protestant church?"

"Yes, it is."

"What was the reason?"

I told him the whole story, and he then asked, "Did you say Mass and give Communion"

"No. I did his regular Sunday worship service. I felt that since you encourage us to exchange pulpits as a show of unity every January, I thought the bishop would be thrilled if I really helped out a Protestant pastor in a time of real need."

That ended the conversation.

Already a little over a year of my stay at Saint Patrick's had gone by, and during the second year a very kind priest came to help me by offering one of the Masses on Sunday. His name was Father

Harry Flynn. He had been the rector of Mount Saint Mary's Seminary in Emmetsburg, Maryland, before coming back to his home diocese in Albany. At the time, he was living at the chancery. He was a big help on Sundays and I was happy to have some wholesome priestly companionship. Harry gave beautiful sermons and when I got a chance I used to listen to him, though I was often busy when he was offering Mass.

One weekend I ran out of altar breads, and on Saturday night I made my own. They were of unleavened bread, and at Mass I had to break the large pieces and give a piece to each person as they come up to receive. I suppose it was much like at the Last Supper, as the large piece was broken and passed around, crumbs fell. I doubt if Jesus concerned himself with picking up the crumbs, though that is what we are supposed to do, out of reverence. I am sure Jesus withdrew his presence from pieces that may have fallen on the floor or on the table. At Father Flynn's Mass, I helped him at Communion time, and after Mass, he quietly went out and picked up the crumbs off the floor. Ashamed, I went out to help him. He was so gracious he never said a word about it, but I learned a lesson to more careful. I now realize that at the Last Supper, when Jesus took the bread and broke it and passed it to those at the table, crumbs fell on the table and on the floor. It is hard for me to imagine him telling the apostles to look for the crumbs that fell and pick them up.

Late into the second year, I felt a need in the parish to have another general confession and absolution. I had been told by the chancellor that he understood my need for it, but whenever I did it I should let them know about it. I had no problem with that. I had the event and again the church was packed, and the remaining stragglers finally came home. I felt so pleased. The whole flock was back together again. The straying sheep were back into the fold. That was my main purpose from my first day in the parish, to gather together the straying sheep. It was a wonderful feeling to see them in church and at Mass in the following weeks. Whereas the church had so many empty seats when I went there two years earlier, the pews were all filled now and at all the Masses.

I sent my letter to the chancery telling them I had general confession and absolution, and I got a letter three days later, telling me that the bishop was very upset, ordering me not to do it again, and to observe not just the spirit of the law but the letter of the law as well. I cannot express my anger at the hypocrisy of that action. When Father Flynn came down that Sunday, I told him about the letter, and he said they were talking about that at the chancery, and they told him that the only reason they sent me the letter was because I wrote and told them what I had done. I did not tell Harry that the chancellor told me that what I was doing was all right, but that I should write and tell them whenever I had to do it. I felt I had really been set up, and knew from that action that I could never trust them again.

In late spring of that year, Harry was made bishop of a diocese in Louisiana, and years later became Archbishop of Minneapolis-Saint Paul archdiocese. By that time, the pressure for me to write a book about Jesus was bothering my conscience so much because I had been postponing it for over four years. I knew I had to make a decision to do something. As long as I was in a parish, I could not write. It was just too busy. I finally decided that if I was going to do what God wanted me to do, and write a book that would make Jesus real for people, I was going to have to resign from the priesthood. That broke my heart even to think of it, but I felt I had no choice. I made my decision, and had made up my mind that I would tell the bishop the very next day.

However, before I got a chance, early the next morning, my doctor called. He had never called me before. I always had to call him. He said he wanted to see me as soon as possible. I asked him what it was about and he said he would tell me when I got there. So, I went to his office immediately, and he began to tell me what was on his mind. "I have been analyzing your tests and all your records, and they look pretty grim. Your blood pressure is out of control, your cholesterol is very high, and your red blood cell count is making your blood too thick. Now what that all means is this; your high blood pressure constricts your blood vessels; your thick blood has a difficult time traveling through your constricted blood vessels and the cholesterol forms a net trapping your blood from flowing freely. The stress caused by your work is killing you, and if we don't do something about it, the way your records show, you probably will be dead by Christmas. So, what do you intend to do about it?"

My temptation was not to take him seriously, as I didn't feel sick, and I had no pains, and no symptoms, so, jokingly, I said, "Suppose I just retire and write books."

His response was, "That would be the best thing you could do. Otherwise, you will not be alive much longer. The combination of medical problems that you have is fatal, and I am not just trying to frighten you."

I did not know how to feel. I was faced with the honest prospect that my life was on the brink of coming to an end. I had no money, just a few thousand dollars in the bank. What would I do for income? But, then, I thought that if I retired for health reasons, the bishop would then have to allow me to function as a priest. And I would now be free to write about Jesus and still practice my priesthood. So, I left the office with very mixed feelings. Before I left, the doctor gave me strict instructions as to what I absolutely had to do to try to reverse the complicated medical issues I was suffering from. My diet had to be severely restricted. I had to get exercise every day. I had to avoid all stress, and any situations that could be stressful.

As soon as I got back to the rectory, the full force of what Doctor Tony Kelly told me, hit home. I was going to die, and maybe within six months. His instructions as to what I had to do were depressing. I loved doing my own cooking and I loved to eat. I sat down and wrote a letter to the bishop telling him that the doctor told me that I had to retire. I sent it out immediately.

After waiting for almost a month, I decided that the chancery was not going to answer my letter, so I wrote another letter telling the bishop that by July, he should have a priest assigned to the parish as I would be gone by then. I got a phone the very next day. The bishop wanted to see me.

When I went to the chancery, he was pleasant enough. At first he asked me not to retire, but to take a leave of absence for six months. I said that that was out of the question as it would put me in another stressful position to have to make another decision in six months, and the doctor already told me that I might be dead by then.

"Well, I don't want you freelancing, like the military chaplains do when they come home."

"Bishop, I don't want to do anything more or less than what any retired priest is allowed to do."

Then, realizing what his real problem was, that because my young age, if he allowed me to retire with a pension, or some kind of compensation, he was afraid that other priests might try to do the same thing. So, I told him, "Bishop, if you are worried about the money, I don't want any."

"Oh, all right then." So, that was our agreement. He let me function as a priest as I was not going to be a financial liability to the diocese.

With that I left the chancery. I had the feeling that when he told the chancery staff, they all let out a big sigh of relief. I know I had been very difficult for them to deal with, but I had told those years before that I did not want to be a pastor, and I know I had been a thorn in their hearts the whole time I was pastor. I am sure no priest ever gave them so much trouble, and I could not blame them for the way they felt about me. I am sure they were just glad to get rid of me. The previous bishop had told some of my old Carmelite classmates that he wished he could get rid of me, as I was a thorn in his heart. I tried so hard to be a good priest that my superiors could be proud of and I had failed miserably, and was walking out into a void that frightened me, not proud of any notable accomplishments in my superiors' eyes, but as an insufferable nuisance.

The people in the parish were so gracious and supportive. They had a wonderful retirement party for me, although I never liked people making a fuss over me just for doing my job. We had some teary goodbyes. I loved those people who were so appreciative of what we were able to do together in only two years. I hoped my stay made a permanent difference. I was still on the board of directors for Senior Projects of Ravena, which ran the programs for the elderly, the congregate meals, the delivered meals to the shut-ins each day, and the other services. I would have to go to their meetings every month, and eventually the program had accumulated enough money from our investments that we were able to finance the construction of a senior citizen center where all the programs for the elderly were administered from then on as an independent entity, no longer a part of the parish, and it is still thriving today, 30 years later.

When I left the parish, it was with a box of good wishes. One card struck me. It was from a Protestant lady, congratulating me on my new ministry. I called and told her I was retiring because of my health. She said, "Your ministry is just beginning and it is going to be worldwide." I thanked her for her kind wishes, and said nothing more.

When I left I didn't know where to go. I finally went to my parents' house as a first stop, and the pickup truck that followed me dropped off all my possessions. There wasn't much, mostly books and my research microscope, and camera equipment I once used for science work when I was a monk. I think I put them in the cellar temporarily, and told my mother and father that I had other things in mind so it would be only temporary. I lied. I didn't know where to go or what to do. After a few days, my sister Margaret Mary told me I could stay at her house. So, I got all my things together and in stages brought everything up to her place which was about six miles away, and put most of my books in her garage which she was not using.

She was a gift from God, and I will always be grateful for her kindness. I know it was not easy for her. She was not used to having big brother around. But, she was kind and understanding. I know I was sloppy as I was continually working on manuscripts and was not too orderly. The space was limited and as my needs for more space grew, my sloppiness became more evident, yet she put up with it.

One day, Regina Chicorelli, who inherited a funeral business from her husband, had an unoccupied bungalow out on Kenwood Avenue in the farmland south of Albany, in an area called Slingerlands. She was kind enough to let me live there. She used to have a lot of funerals at Saint Patrick's in Ravena, and we had become good friends. She never charged me rent for my stay in the house, but I always paid her something, and gradually increased it as I was later able to. Though the house was not furnished, except for a bed, there was wall to wall carpeting, and the house was comfortable and in excellent condition. Next to the house was a radio station, and although I did not have a radio I could hear their music coming through the electrical socket on the wall in each room.

I bought one chair. It was a nice arm chair with blue velour upholstery, and very comfortable. As furniture was too costly, I bought some wood and made my own table and chair. I had a wooden bowl I got from a missionary, as a sample of the work at their mission, and I had a plastic plate from a TV dinner, and a few necessary utensils. It was like starting life from scratch, and it was fun. There was no need for anyone to feel sorry for me; I was having the time of my life, the happiest years I ever had. The reason for the few dishes and utensils and lack of furniture was due to the fact that, not long after I retired, someone very close asked if I could help him, and I gave him what I had in the bank. They needed it more than I did, as they had a family, so the decision was simple. I never needed much, and I enjoyed the simplicity of this new life.

My only need was food basically, though I did have to pay the chancery for my medical insurance, which amounted to a little less than four hundred dollars a month. Fortunately, Father Paul Bondi the pastor at the church in Ballston Spa asked me to offer a Mass on the weekends, and the stipend for that covered the medical insurance bill. Also, I was still on the Independent Review Board for the State, and Niagara Mohawk Power Company's advisory board, and the mileage money was a help for whatever other expenses I had. Gas was a lot cheaper then, so my only other bills were for food, and whatever little I paid in rent to Mrs. Chicorelli.

When it came to food, I was at first depressed at the prospect because I knew I had to follow a strict diet, so one day I went to the supermarket and walked up and down each aisle, reading label after label, trying to see just what was healthy, and acceptable. I thought I would be disappointed, but, on the contrary, I found that there were a lot of things I could eat, so I made a mental list of all those things and went home and started to make my own recipes with all the allowable ingredients. Fruit and fresh vegetables were essential, but they were getting costly. The vegetables and melons I could buy from the neighbors who had the farm across the street.

Their prices were always reasonable, and the family were good friends as well as good neighbors.

When I moved to this new place, there was already a telephone in the house, which I activated. It was a great relief going through a day without phone calls, and without the usual stress that they often entailed. I thought I might miss all the people calling, but the peace and quiet was a great blessing. The silence all day long, and having practically no contact with people was like being back in the monastery, though now more like a Carthusian monastery, or a Camaldolese monastery where you lived alone and grew your own food on a little plot of land alongside your cell. My little garden was fun and I grew a lot of my vegetables, but had to fight the squirrels that were continually digging up the seedlings, and just leaving them lying on the ground. My garden, however, I didn't start until the next spring because it was too late the first year I moved there.

In trying to eat healthy, I decided to bake my own bread. With five pounds of flour I could make five loaves of bread and save money. My first attempt, however, was a total failure, though not really a total failure because I ended up eating my failure. I decided to bake whole wheat bread, so I used whole wheat flour, only. I could not understand why it wouldn't rise, so I figured it would rise when I baked it, which it never did. When it was finally baked, I took it out of the oven, and it looked just the same as it did when I put it in. I tried to cut a slice. My knife was not very sharp, but I figured it could at least cut a piece of bread. It couldn't. I finally decided that I was not going to waste a whole loaf of bread. So, I brought it down to the cellar where I had a band saw, and cut it up in thin slices, and used it as crackers for little pieces of blue cheese and jalapeño peppers, four of which I allowed me to indulge in every night. I found out that when you make whole wheat bread, you use only a small amount of whole wheat flour, mixed with a much higher ratio of ordinary flour

When I first retired, my brother Edward, with whom I was always close since childhood, and who had been a psychotherapist all his working life, was concerned that my having to retire at such a young age could have a damaging effect on me psychologically, so he insisted I make an appointment with a psychiatrist. I didn't feel I needed to; I thought I had proved myself when I functioned well in the parish I just left, but I made my appointment and went for my first session, after which he scheduled another. When I went back for the second session, I was hardly with the man for five minutes, when he told me, "Father, you are so healthy it's a waste of time for you to come here. Go, and enjoy your life." That was a relief. At least I knew I was still sane, though I knew others doubted it.

When summer came, I continued my custom of taking my Mom and Dad on vacation. Thank God I had a couple of credit cards. Usually we traveled cross country, and on our way back home, almost always went to Williamsburg, Virginia, which we all loved because of its cultural and historical richness. My father loved it particularly, because his hero, Thomas Jefferson, played so much a part in the early life of our country. He loved the movie they showed in the visitor center, "The Story of a Patriot," so I decided to buy it for him, and put it on my credit card. My father warned against having those things, and predicted that they would one day ruin the American economy. On the way home we visited Monticello. Early American history and especially the United States Constitution were things my father was intensely interested in. He had read and pondered the Constitution so many times, I think he had it memorized. He also studied the life and thinking of Thomas Jefferson, and had a good sense of his political philosophy. This was interesting because my father never went past the sixth grade in school. It would have been interesting to think of what he could have been if he had had an education, but he contented himself, and mother, too, to make sure we had a chance for a good education.

His knowledge of the Constitution was not just a theoretical exercise. For him it had practical implications, especially concerning rights of children in parochial schools. It convinced him that the government's denial of busing and textbooks for children in private religious schools was unconstitutional, and with the help of lawyers from the New York State Catholic Conference, he went to Washington with my brother Edmund and challenged the law before the United States Supreme Court. When they came back home, he told mother that judging from the questions the justices asked, he was sure he was going to win the case, which, as was announced shortly afterwards, he did. From that time on students in religious schools could ride the school buses to and from their schools. Not much later, the textbook law was passed providing textbooks on secular subjects to students in religious schools. We were proud of him. Whoever would have thought?

That all happened years before, but it was our visits to Williamsburg that had intensified his understanding of the Constitution. And even those long trips out west and down south were a thing of the past, as my mother could no longer stand the hot, humid weather down south, and out west. It put too much pressure on her already weak heart, so I started taking my parents to Maine, where we just relaxed. We found a place in Booth Bay Harbor, I think it was opposite the harbor, in South Booth Bay, where there was a very nice motel owned by the Barnes family. We stayed there for a few weeks and had a wonderful time. It was there that I started to write "Joshua." I wrote the first part of the manuscript by hand, and got a few chapters done while my Mom and Dad took a nap in the afternoon. When I was writing the manuscript, I had the eeriest feeling that my whole past life with its very complicated and strange happenings was a training process God had been putting me through to provide me with the knowledge and experience I needed to write this manuscript about Jesus. With it also went the premonition that when I finished it, I was going to die, as that book was the purpose of my life. I began to think back. It was odd being so focused on Jesus and Communion every morning, ever since childhood, and a need to learn more about him as I grew.

Even in my theology courses, I used to integrate the theological concepts with Jesus' thinking, before they could make sense to me. And then as I got older, I felt a restless need to write about Him. For so many years this need haunted me, and finally I had the peace in knowing that I was at last doing what I knew for so long God had intended that I do.

After that vacation in the cool, refreshing ocean air, we came back home refreshed and invigorated. I was so happy to provide those little vacation spaces for my parents. Raising us twelve kids was not easy, and I could only imagine the worry and stress involved especially as each of us was becoming a teenager. To see the both happy and relaxed on vacation was my joy, and I never regretted having spent all my vacations with them. They were never boring; my father's wit and humor constantly entertained us, and mother's secretly praying the rosary as I was driving, saved our lives more than once, and that is not just pious interpretation of events.

The following summer we drove up to Maine again, but this time we had decided before we left home, that we would take the ferry over to Nova Scotia. That was fun. We arrived late in the afternoon, and went directly to the motel, and got a good sleep. The next morning, we had Mass in the motel room as we did every morning before we went down to breakfast. It was always such a healing and comforting way to start each day. The area was still primitive, much like Cape Cod would have been a hundred years ago. What was impressive was the beautiful and gigantic wooden churches, all painted white. What a job that must be to have to paint them every few years! But, family life there is centered on church, so I am sure it was a whole parish event keeping the church in good condition. While there is not much to do in Nova Scotia, there were provincial parks all along the coast particularly on the western coast. We never needed any entertainment. We kept each other entertained. Mother was always famous for her stories, which meant a lot to me because I had been away from home since I was 14, and had been home only occasionally after that and never for very long, so I never had a chance to get to know my brothers and sisters. From all the stories Mother told me on vacation, I got to know each one of them and learned to understand them through Mother's eyes and heart. In this way, I learned to love each one of them in a special way that I could not have done if I had lived with them through the years. The stories she told, however, made me wish I could have been a part of their life during all those years. During the trip to Wyoming they told me stories about the family, but interestingly, now the stories were all new and different from the ones they told me previously.

As Mother told these stories and Dad added his humor to each one about each of my brothers and sisters, I got a pretty good picture of what life at home was like. Then as lunch or supper time approached, we stopped at a nearby provincial park and had our picnics by the ocean every day, with food Dad brought with him in his Styrofoam picnic containers. He always managed to find dry ice to keep the food frozen for most of our time away. And as he always had such a variety, our meals were always something we looked forward to. We had so much fun. It brings tears to my eyes as I write this, knowing that those days will never happen again, but thank God that they could happen and did happen at one time which now seems so very long ago.

Chapter Nineteen

Once back home I could not wait to continue working on the manuscript. The progress on it was rapid, since I felt my whole life had been a preparation for it. Once I started it, I worked continually until I finished it. What to do with it became the problem. I knew there would be no way a publisher would accept it, and I knew I could not even afford to send out copies of the manuscript to a large list of agents, so my only alternative was to have it printed by a reputable book printing company. I went to a local printer and asked how much it would cost to print so many copies of the book. For 5000 copies, it would be $15,000. And how much time would they give me to pay the bill? Two months was the response, and if I put the manuscript on a computer disk, I could cut the cost of typesetting from $12.00 a page to $4.00 a page. I decided to go along with that. Now, I had to get a computer, something I knew nothing about. I checked computer stores. Most salespeople knew little more about them than I did. One of my sisters, who has a personality like an uncorked bottle of champagne, mentioned to her husband that I was looking for a computer. He and his father had set up the computers for the Times Union, the Hearst newspaper in Albany. He suggested I get an Olivetti computer, which at the time was the only computer that ran on a 16 bit processor. All the others were eight bit. As there was no Olivetti person I knew of in the area to help me, I called the Olivetti Company in Tarrytown,

New York, and asked if I could become a dealer. They were delighted and signed me up for their training program to teach me all about their computer and Olivetti printers. My strategy was to have access to their technicians, and the only way I could have that, was if I was one of their dealers. Long story short was that I became one of their top dealers nationwide, only because I sold them for cost, as all I really wanted was one for myself. As a top dealer, I won a trip for two to Monte Carlo and Paris. I had no interest in going, but I knew my cousin George Cinney, who had been my best friends since we were kids, would be interested. But, all that is way ahead of the story and totally irrelevant to anything, except that it was fun, especially since it was tied up with a trip to the Holy Land with a few other friends at the same time. The Dominican Third Order group for whom I was their director, asked if I would be their guide. Since guides went free, I couldn't say no, so I agreed. They were four people short however, so I asked some people from Ravena, who years before asked if they could go on a trip to the Holy Land sometime with me. They were only too happy. However, the original group decided not to go, because of the Intifada that summer, so I was now committed to the four from Ravena. At that point I decided that I would call my cousin George Cinney and ask if he was interested. He was thrilled. In this way, we combined both the trip to the Holy Land and the trip to Monte Carlo and Paris. We did have a wonderful time. The group from Ravena returned home after we left the Holy Land and arrived in Rome, while George and I continued touring Italy, which was no problem for George financially, nor for me thanks to my credit card and George's generosity. The $500 dollars in cash I had saved was long gone, and I wanted to carry at least some share of my expenses.

We visited every worthwhile site in Rome including the Catacombs of Saint Sebastian on the Appian Way, where George walked behind a guy you kept sneezing. Immediately I knew that could end up being a big problem, and it sure was. From Rome, we went to Assisi, and then to Venice and to Milan and worked our way to Monte Carlo. When we arrived at Monte Carlo and caught up with the Olivetti group, I wasn't quite ready for that. The waitresses were all topless, and same with the beach on the Riviera. George wasn't feeling well, not because of that as he had a good time with his camera, but because he felt it hard to breathe, but held out until we got to Paris, where he came down with pneumonia. However, we did have a good time. I think it was the bottle of brandy I got him that served as an excellent antibiotic and apparently took care of most of the pneumonia germs so we could enjoy seeing the sights and take nice side trips.

His health held up until we got back home a few days later, when the doctor had to treat him for pneumonia which apparently had come back.

When we got back home from the trip, I had the manuscript of "Joshua" already on the computer disk, and was supposed to send it over by phone to the printing company's printer. This was something I knew nothing about, so a dear friend, Jim McGuinness, of McGuinness Associates, in Schenectady, bailed me out and sent it on his computer. The printing company called back and told me that their printer had already printed the book with the precise font type I specified, and they were ready to make copies, and asked if I would stop over to decide on all the other details of the book's production. I went over to the printing company, and made a design for the cover and picked a high quality hard cover, and the best paper, and the best binding so it would last. They then went ahead and printed the 5000 copies. Those original copies still look like new even though they have been read numerous times.

Fortunately, by that time I had been invited to give retreats at the Dominican Retreat House in Schenectady, and at the Dominican Sisters Retreat House in Elkins Park, Pennsylvania, so whenever I conducted retreats at both those places, "Joshua" was available, and sold very well. Since the retreatants had time to read the book over the weekend, they liked it enough to buy multiple copies for their friends and relatives. Both retreat houses did the same thing. Before long many of those books went to different parts of the United States and I was soon getting orders from all over the country. By the end of the two months, I had all the money I needed to pay the cost of printing the 5000 copies. Within a matter of a few months, I was getting orders from other countries. One of the orders was from Italy, from a bookstore called Libreria Ancora. They ordered a case. I did not know what the Libreria Ancora was until I got their check, which was from the Vatican

Bank, so I knew the book was circulating around the Vatican. To this day, I am told the books are still their most popular sellers in the Vatican bookstore, and are frequently in their front window. They also ship the books to Catholic bookstores in other countries.

When the books first started to sell, Joey Della Ratta, my godson, used to help me. We had an order one day which shocked him. "Fahd, look at this order. It's from Hindu monks in India. They want a whole case of "Joshua" for their libraries. How do you know them, Fahd?"

"I don't know them, Joe. I guess God wants Jesus known over there, too."

I didn't have the slightest idea how they even found out about the book. The only thing I could figure was that since "Joshua" had been recommended in the "American Journal of Psychiatry," and a good number of local Hindus who are in that field were reading "Joshua," they may have recommended it to family and friends back in India and the word spread.

After three years, I was so tired of packing books and typing invoices, I never had a chance to write. Fortunately, my sister Lorraine was a wonderful help to me at the time. At the end of the three years over 50,000 copies had sold. Thank God, help came to free me from publishing and marketing. One day I got a phone call from an agent, Peter Ginsberg, telling me he had read "Joshua" and was deeply moved by it, and wondered if I needed an agent. I gladly told him I would love to have an agent. So, I signed a contract with his company, Curtis Brown, Ltd., of which he was the president, and within a short time Macmillan Publishing Company sent a contract, which Peter had negotiated with them for the paperback edition which came out a short time later.

It was interesting that 28 publishers had turned it down. Macmillan was one of them, then one day a lady from Doubleday, named Michelle Rapkin, went to work at Macmillan, and Peter called her and mentioned "Joshua," suggesting that she read it. She did and loved it, and gave it to Barry Lippman, the publisher, who told her to get that book no matter what it cost, which she did. After processing "Joshua" for publication, (and that was all that Michelle did at Macmillan), she went back to Doubleday. Soon Joshua was selling in the hundreds of thousands and now after well over 25 years is still selling. Michelle once remarked that she never had the slightest idea why she went to Macmillan. She felt that she was supposed to be there for some reason, and once she was settled in, all she did was "Joshua," then left and went back to Doubleday. Fortunately, Joshua also had an excellent publicist in Susan Richman who had been with Macmillan for many years and knew everyone worthwhile around the country whom she could contact for support, which made the sales skyrocket. She was remarkable, a one woman public relations operation. It was very interesting that everyone involved in the publication of this book about Jesus were Jewish. It seems they were chosen to spread Jesus' message around the world.

The immediate popularity of the book, created demand for talks and tours, and my life became busier than ever. Fortunately, I had been slowly recuperating from my debilitating weakness, and was able to travel and give talks, something which I thought I would never be able to do since I had been so frightfully weak for the first two years right after I retired. Fortunately, my sister Lorraine was a tremendous help to me once I started to travel on book tours and speaking engagements. She took care in a most efficient manner of all that had to be done in the office, filling orders for books and shipping them. Later on , her husband Lester and her son Joe came up to help and I could never thank them enough for all their support. Whenever I tried to give them something for all their help they would never accept it.

In time, we decided to have Doubleday as our publisher. Since then, for the past 15 years, Trace Murphy had been not only my editor, but a most gracious and staunch supporter of what I can only call my ministry of making Jesus better known throughout the world. I look upon him and Peter as my co-apostles, my Luke and Mark. I don't know where I would be without their constant support, and wise counsel.

"I always felt that writing
about Jesus
and making him real to people was
a healthy way of showing
graphically how desperately
Jesus is needed today."

Chapter Twenty

Early after Joshua began to circulate; I began to get letters from hundreds of people from all over the world. Many of the letters were from people with very difficult problems. One of the first letters I received was from a 90 year old Poor Clare nun. She wrote and told me had been a nun for over 65 years, and that she had read Joshua, and after reading it, for the first time in her life she felt comfortable being a Catholic. Soon after that I received a phone call from five girls in the sixth grade. "Hello, is this Father Girzone?

"Yes, it is." "We are five girls in the sixth grade. We just finished reading Joshua, and we wanted to tell you how much we loved it and that we all fell in love with Jesus. Thank you very much," and she hung up. I was so frustrated because I had a thousand questions to ask her. But, that was the typical reaction, people telling me that they had fallen in love with Jesus.

A Jewish man called one day and asked if he could meet with me. We met. He was a man in his late seventies. After talking for a while he told me that his ancestors built the first synagogue in Albany. He went on to tell me that after reading Joshua, he recognized him as the Jesus he always pictured in his mind, and then went on to say, "But what have our people, ours as well as yours, what have we done to that beautiful, beautiful man?"

Some letters were from Central and South America, a number of them from families of dictators, telling me that after reading Joshua they went and started building orphanages for the children roaming the streets. Some were from bishops telling me how much they disliked the book. One bishop said it was "overly simplistic." Many were from just ordinary people, mostly people who had been hurting, and telling me that after reading the book, they came back to Church. An unusually large number of priests wrote and told me Joshua saved their priesthood. Many letters were from Southern Baptists who wrote and told me that after meeting Joshua they found a Jesus so different from the Jesus they were taught, a Jesus who healed them and lifted burdens they had carried all their life. They told me that they felt guilty because they could not fall in love with the Jesus in the gospel stories, but fell in love with Jesus in Joshua, because he was a real flesh and blood Jesus, the kind of Jesus they always dreamed about.

So many of the letters were from people who had been addicted to drugs or alcohol for years and after reading Jesus their whole life changed and they had been free of drug ever since. Many of the letters were invitations to speak in places as far away as South Africa, and Germany, and in South America.

One of the most interesting letters was from an international tax lawyer in Belgium. He told me he had a dream one night, and in the dream, saw a maroon colored book with a title that appeared to be with a Jewish name on the cover. A voice told him to get it and read it. (At the time, my first edition was a maroon colored hardcover with the name Joshua on the front.) The man, his name was Michael Devlin, told me that at first he paid no attention because it was only a dream, but shortly afterwards he had to go to Florida, and while there went into a bookstore, and his eyes immediately caught sight of a maroon colored book on the shelf with the word Joshua on it. It was the same book he saw in the dream, and he heard the words, "That's the book, get it and read it." He bought the book, brought it back to the hotel, and read it. Shortly afterwards he ordered a case of the books, forty-eight copies, and brought them back to Belgium with him, where they circulated throughout the American Catholic parish attached to Louvain University, and among parishioners among whom were people attached to NATO headquarters and the various embassies, and to people in the European Parliament, and various corporations.

Shortly after that Mike's pastor invited me to speak at their church. I accepted and flew over to Belgium, and was warmly welcomed. I was scheduled to give a series of five talks in five successive evenings beginning the following Monday. The day the talks were to begin, the pastor told me that he would be surprised if there would be more than a dozen people coming as NATO maneuvers were scheduled to begin and it was a busy week for others besides. A little before seven,11 people had arrived. I felt disappointed, and wish they could have arranged for a better time to come. However, by seven o'clock there were over 250 people, including the NATO people who were supposed to have maneuvers that week. Besides that, there were people from the European Parliament and ambassadors and officials of various multinational corporations stationed there. And up to 300 came each of the following nights. To this day, the Devlins, who now live near Boston, are close friends, together with wonderful friend, Marlis de Rozairo, who came to the talks in Waterloo, and still, 25 years later, comes to my talks in America.

It turned out to be a very successful week. It was an entirely new Jesus who had been presented to them that week, an understanding that was scripturally and theologically sound, but a Jesus who healed and lifted many burdens of so many of them. To them it was a Jesus they hoped was the Jesus they dreamed of in their hearts but not the Jesus that they had preached to them all their lives. I made friends there who after all these years are still dear friends. Mike and Elie Devlin, who introduced me to those people, now live in Massachusetts, not far from where I presently live, and Elie was kind enough to stop off for a brief visit recently, when bringing her young son to Albany for his bar exams.

That talk in Waterloo, was the beginning of a whole series of talks across the United States, and Canada, and Australia, Honolulu, and China. Fortunately, due to my rigid regimen of exercise and strict diet, my health had improved to the point where I could take on this strenuous ministry. I finally felt like I was being a priest again by preaching Jesus and making him better known throughout the world, and not only to Catholics, but also to Jews, Hindus, and people of other beliefs as well as those with no particular belief. It was a wonderful ministry. What was so surprising was the numbers of people and the variety of people who came. Often the majority was not Catholic, and the response was always the same. "We feel as if we have met the real Jesus for the first time in the Jesus you present to us. We always hoped that Jesus would be the way you presented him in your talk, but we never heard anybody talk about Jesus like that, and it is so healing."

Early in this ministry I was invited to Oconomowoc, Wisconsin, by Jack and Karen Swanson. Karen's family owned the Miller Brewing Company. They had a beautiful home on the lake, and for years had been taking in children with problems and raised and educated them. Jack and Karen were among the first to embrace Joshua, and introduce him to many of their friends. They arranged for me to give a talk in Milwaukee, which was attended by Archbishop Rembert Weakland, as well as a good number clergy of various denominations. Father Joe Hunt, a former Benedictine monk, who had presently been teaching Hebrew at Nashotah House, introduced me, and told the people how much Joshua had helped him. Father Joe had at one time been a consultant to Pope Paul VI on the Hebrew Scriptures, called by many the Old Testament.

After the talk, I asked him what a scholar like him could get out of a simple book like Joshua. His response was, "You will never know how that book has helped me to understand what Jesus is all about.

That book ministers to me like no other book I have ever read. I have read Joshua nine times so far. I read it every morning with my Bible."

Archbishop Weakland was most gracious and very encouraging. We became good friends during that visit and two following visits to Oconomowoc for talks in the area. As I got to know him, especially from his books and from a talk he gave at the Los Angeles Congress where we both gave talks on two separate days. I was impressed with the depth and breadth of his understanding of the Church and its mission in the world. I wished there were more bishops like him. He was without doubt one of the most brilliant bishops in the country.

One day I received letter from a Southern Baptist theologian, Doctor John Killinger asking me if I would come to Samford University in Birmingham, Alabama, to speak about Jesus. Samford was a fundamentalist stronghold, and was dubbed the "Buckle of the Bible Belt." I accepted Doctor Killinger's invitation and worked it out in conjunction with a talk I had to give in Mississippi. My talk in Mississippi was scheduled for the day before the talk I was to give in Birmingham.

Then something strange and quite disturbing happened, something which was to happen on other occasions, and made me realize that there was something trying to obstruct my preaching about Jesus, and that there was a counter force trying to protect me along the way. It was becoming more and more evident. The morning after

I spoke in Mississippi, the pastor drove me around to see the sights. Before we had gotten very far he remembered he had forgotten something, so we went back to the rectory to get it. When we arrived, there was a car in the driveway. It turned out to be a man who works for an airline and also helps the priest with what has to be done on the computer. When we went inside, the man said, "Isn't Father Girzone scheduled for a flight to Birmingham on such and such an airline?" "Yes, why?" "That airline just declared bankruptcy. But, don't worry about it, I can make arrangements for him to get there, but he'll have to take a flight to Atlanta first." So, that's what I did. Those little interesting coincidences! That man wasn't scheduled to be at the rectory that morning and just happened to go to work on the computer. The airline declared bankruptcy just a couple of hours earlier. And the man happened to be working for an airline and knew just how to arrange for a flight to Birmingham. That was just one of many incidents similar that seemed very strange, but always worked out in the last minute as if there was a chess game being played behind the scenes.

When I arrived in Birmingham, Doctor Killinger met me at the airport and we became friends immediately, together with all his family. The next morning the auditorium was packed, almost two thousand people. John had done a marvelous job promoting the event. I was surprised at how quiet the crowd was especially since I spoke for two hours. Again, it made me realize how hungry people are to learn about Jesus. Afterwards as John and I were walking along the campus, people stopped us and said, "You'll never know what you did by coming here."

"Why, what did I do?"

"You gave us Jesus."

"What do you mean, I gave you Jesus? You people are experts in the Scriptures."

"Well, we may have studied Scripture all our lives but we never got to know Jesus, and you gave a flesh and blood Jesus who has healed wounds and lifted burdens from our hearts that we had carried all our life."

I was humbled, because it took a lot for a Southern Baptist minister to say that to Roman Catholic priest, but it shows how much we crave what Jesus has to give us, and rarely do people really hear anything with any depth about Jesus. When they do they are stunned and I think that explained the eerie silence in that huge auditorium for a whole two hours. And this was the experience everyplace I went, showing how hungry people are to hear about Jesus which they hardly ever hear in their churches because clergy rarely know enough about Jesus to say much about him, other than commenting on chapter and verse on gospel stories. I have read books by so many theologians, among them some of my favorite theologians, and it is hard to believe, few discuss in any depth Jesus' relationships with people, and one wrote a beautiful book about Jesus and never once wrote anything about relationships in

Jesus' life. In fact, he didn't even mention the word. That says volumes.

Many years after Joshua was published, a friend translated Joshua into Japanese. It began immediately to circulate around the country. Koji Yamazaki, my friend, did a masterful job on the translation, according to a Japanese priest who was taking graduate theology and scripture courses in Chicago. The CEO of IBM Japan bought a hundred copies and gave them as presents to his CEO friends, and they all commented after reading it that even though they were Buddhists and Shintoists, they fell in love with Jesus, and they didn't realize that the book was about Jesus until they finished it, and they said that by then it was too late, because they had already fallen in love with him. This merely illustrates that whatever it is that Jesus has, the whole world craves it, and once they find him, it affects them to the core of their being.

And this phenomenon I have heard expressed over and over, and by so many people, and for various reasons, that it perplexed me, as I could never imagine falling in love with anyone by just reading a book. And yet highly intelligent people were among those who expressed that same sentiment, namely, that they had fallen in love with Jesus after reading Joshua. That same comment meant most to me when I received a letter from a group of Southern Baptists who told me they felt guilty after reading Joshua, because they fell in love with Jesus, something they were never able to do by reading Scripture all their life.

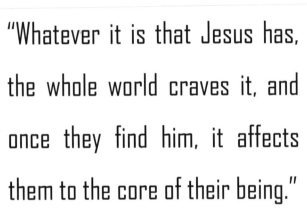

"Whatever it is that Jesus has, the whole world craves it, and once they find him, it affects them to the core of their being."

Chapter Twenty-One

Realizing that I wasn't going to die after all, I began to write another manuscript, "Joshua and the Children," this time putting Joshua in Northern Ireland. The book became a national best seller, and in a matter of a few weeks was on the New York Times best seller list, and stayed there for at least two months. That was interesting because Joshua had sold a 1,000,000 copies by that time and had never made the New York Times best seller list, which made me wonder about the list, as another author, with whom I grew up, told me that his book got on the New York Times best seller list after selling only 5 thousand copies.

Epilogue

During the years since I was first made pastor, so many problems kept arising that priests who knew me often asked why I never left the priesthood, or the Church. I never talked about my life with them, but they knew from rumors spreading around the diocese. Also, informed lay people said the same thing, that if they were treated the way I was they would have left the Church long before.

Even later when "Joshua" came out and spread around the country, prompting people to request speaking engagements all over, the same issue came up after the talks. The large crowds consisting of people of all denominations asked if I ever considered starting my own church. "You would start out with at least 100 thousand members with no trouble at all."

My answer to the lay people as well as to the priests was the same. "That is not an option. Only God can start a religion and tell people how he wants his children to worship him. He started the Jewish religion and set it up with a teaching authority, a magisterium, which Jesus himself recognized in the scribes and Pharisees, and told his disciples to obey, 'because they occupy the chair of Moses, but don't imitate they because they are hypocrites.'

"And Jesus set up the Church as his priceless treasure, which however, is strewn with weeds and smelly fish, and said we should be willing to sacrifice everything to possess it. And he also set up a teaching authority, a magisterium, to teach and administer God's treasures, the sacraments, and promised to be with the Church until the end of time.

At times, however, when the magisterium was not sensitive to God's guidance, God sent prophets to deliver warning messages. As in ancient Israel, so also today, the Holy Spirit uses others to prick the conscience of those entrusted with authority, to prod them into caring for the needs of the flock. It is the responsibility of each individual to make their statement for what is needed.

I always felt that writing about Jesus and making him real to people was a healthy way of showing graphically how desperately Jesus is needed today. But, for me to break away and start my own religion would be totally disloyal to Jesus. I have no authority to start a religion in competition with what God has ordained for us. I have always felt that my job was to encourage shepherds in the Church to be more faithful to the image of the Good Shepherd that Jesus set before us as a model of how we should care for God's hurting sheep. For me to further fragment the flock would be against Jesus' prayer at the Last Supper, 'Father, I pray that they may all be one as you and I are one, so that the world may believe that you have sent me.' To tear apart the Church is to muddle the clear portrait of Jesus that we should mirror to the world. I pray that I will always be loyal to the Church. It is the mystical body of Jesus, and to leave the mystical body of Christ is never an option. It confuses the people and obscures the image of Jesus' presence in the world.

People so often fail to believe Saint Paul when he says that we are all engrafted into the one body of Christ. How do you tear yourself away from the body, without losing identity and dying? The Church will always be to me, as weak and frail and sinful as I may be, Jesus' most precious treasure and greatest gift. It is the living presence of Jesus throughout history.

Quotes on the following pages

Original source 246 Highlighted on 54
Original source 258 Highlighted on 72
Original source 199 Highlighted on100
Original source 265 Highlighted on 113
Original source 261 Highlighted on 180
Original source 264 Highlighted on 196
Original source 254 Highlighted on 208
Original source 269 Highlighted on 256
Original source 265 Highlighted on 266

56126498R00150

Made in the USA
Middletown, DE
13 December 2017